Myra Wood

Crazy Lace

an artistic approach to Creative Lace Knitting

publisher
Woodworks Editions
Sherman Oaks, CA

book editors
Edie Eckman
Ellene Warren
Page Wood

photographers
Cesar Cuevas
Myra Wood

assistant to Mr. Cuevas
Ari Abramczyk

layout & design
Myra Wood

printer
C & C Printing
Hong Kong, China

wardrobe stylist
Anne Edwards,
Anne Richardson Collection

make-up artist
Sharon Hawkey

models
Jill Evyn
Sarah Marie Hilker
Samantha Rea

WW
A Woodworks Editions book
www.myrawood.com

Crazy Lace
an artistic look at creative lace knitting

ISBN-13: 978-0980018288
ISBN-10:0980018285

First publication in 2009 by Woodworks Editions

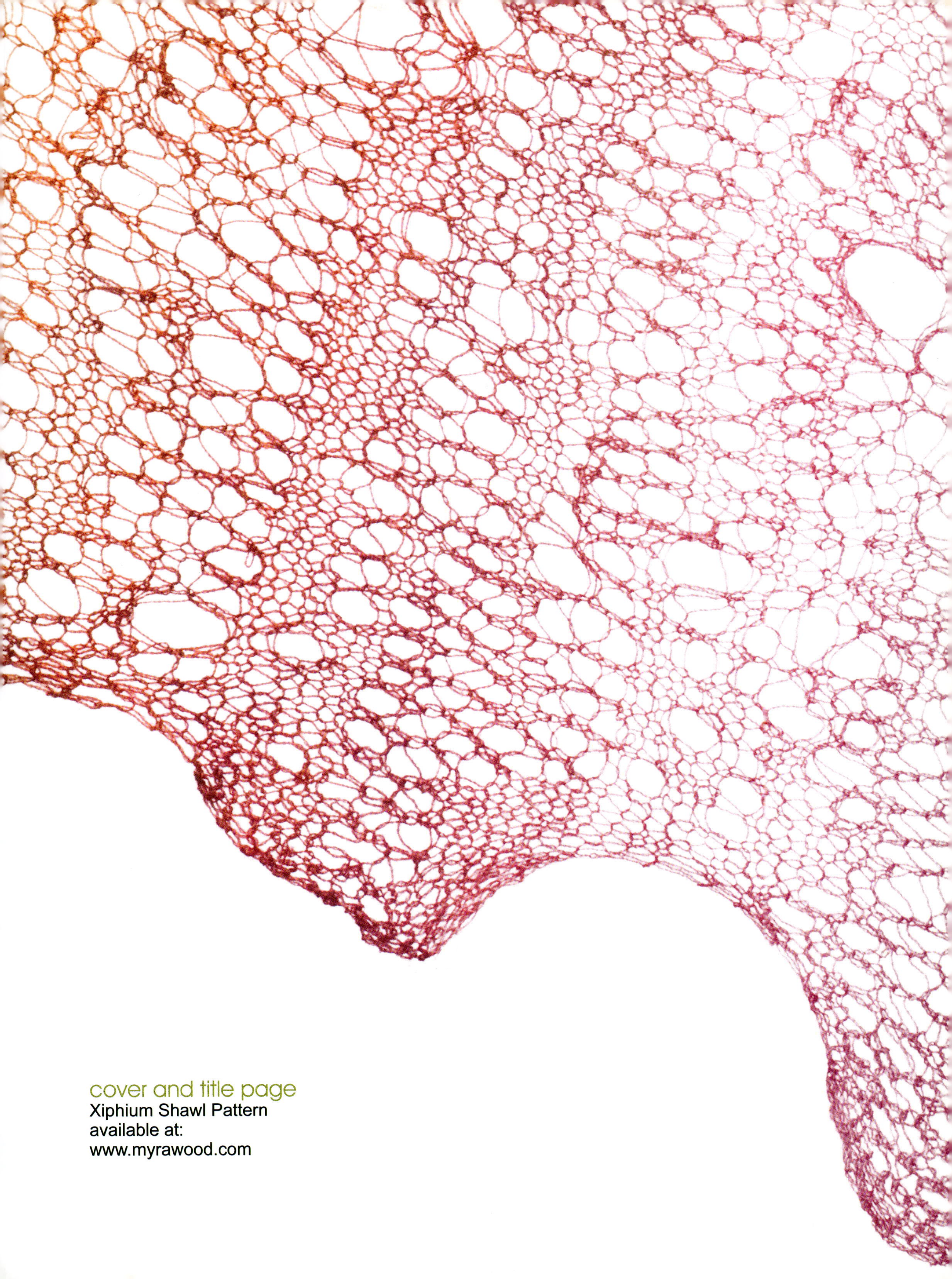

cover and title page
Xiphium Shawl Pattern
available at:
www.myrawood.com

dedication

I'm blessed to live a creative life with the help and inspiration from so many wonderful people every single day. I'm truly grateful and thank you all.

To my husband, Page, my partner, my heart and soul, my life. No words could ever express the depth of my love.

To Ellene Warren, extraordinary soul with wisdom of the ages and best friend a person could ever wish for. You make me wanna be a better woman.

To Annie Edwards, amazingly talented artist, for dressing the models with your gorgeous designs. I'm your biggest fan.

To my family, both biological and freeform, for the unending support and encouragement.

To Cesar Cuevas, incomparable photographer with charm and wit for days. What an eye!

To Jill, Sarah and Sam, thank you for sharing your beauty inside and out.

To Herbert Neibling who started the whole process by making me crazy.

To all of the teachers who share their knowledge of every type of needleart with the world and pay it forward. I'm proud to walk among you.

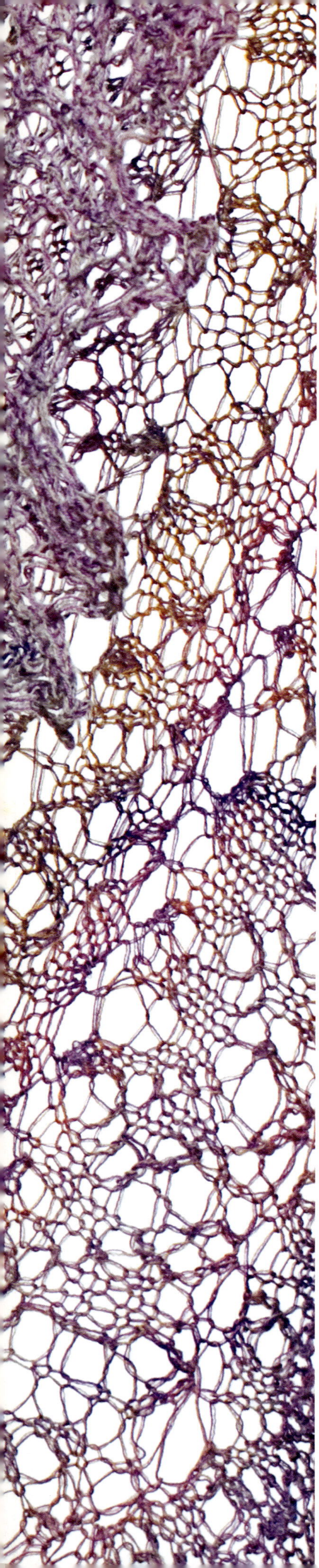

foreword

I have been a knitter for more than 50 years and have loved lace knitting for the last 6 of them. In addition to having a huge collection of lace knitting books and compendiums, I have also published my own patterns for knitted lace garments and accessories.

Lace knitting had always been a slow and painful process for me, fraught with mathematical challenges and involving repeated froggings. That is, until the afternoon Myra showed me some of her original projects for the book you are now holding in your hands, and explained the principles of her new techniques for lace knitting to me. My mind was blown and my fingers literally ached to get started!

Basically, what Crazy Lace did for me was gave me permission to be creative, have fun with lace knitting, think outside the box and enjoy the process! I immediately sat down with the EZ Pi Shawl formula and a bag of gorgeous fingering weight yarn, and in two days I had created a thing of beauty. A 70" wide circular shawl with a saw-toothed edge had simply flowed from my needles without one episode of frustration and without even once having to frog! As I knitted round and round, sometimes placing yarn overs, increases and decreases randomly and sometimes counting out stitches to repeat a pattern, I felt liberated. A few extra stitches at the end of the round? Just knit them! A dropped stitch? Just add one in somewhere else! I never once had to use a calculator and the only time my pencil and paper were employed were to keep track of rounds.

After my last increase round, I counted my stitches and realized I had somehow ended up with 11 less stitches than I was meant to have. In the past, that would have caused me to frog back to the last place I had the correct number of stitches. With over 400 stitches on my needles, that would have caused extreme pain. A couple of episodes like that might have even caused me to abandon the project altogether. Under the influence of Myra's techniques, I merely added the 11 stitches to the next round and happily continued clicking away.

Crazy Lace has changed the way I design lace projects for publication as well. I now can build my own stitch patterns by relating each row or round to the ones before, instead of endlessly searching through my collections of stitch dictionaries for patterns that will fit into a certain number of stitches. Fun instead of pain!

I believe that Crazy Lace will change your relationship to lace knitting for the better, just as it has forever altered mine. Myra's ideas may seem revolutionary to you - because they are! I have never read about or heard of anyone approaching lace knitting in this way, but I am certain of one thing. This book is going to rock your world!
Have fun, enjoy, go Crazy!

Ellene Warren

randomly symmetric
swirl circle shawl
Yarn Place, *Gentle*, laceweight
overdyed with purple hair dye
Size 7/4.5 mm needles

contents

completely random
rectangular stole
with irregular borders
Yarn Place, *Gentle in Marooned*
Size 6/4 mm needles

randomly symmetric
swirl circle shawl
Yarn Place, *Gentle*, laceweight
overdyed with purple hair-dye
Size 7/4.5 mm needles

introduction

Lace patterns can be very intimidating for many new knitters. Seasoned knitters may be comfortable with the technical aspects of knitting lace, but may not always enjoy endless lines of instruction or staring at intricate charts. Although I love knitting of all kinds, especially lace knitting, I found the rigidity of traditional directions frustrated me. I knew there had to be a way to get back to knitting for the joy of knitting and be able to knit lace too.

I'm one of those "what if?" knitters. Being a freeform fiber freak at heart, whenever I start a pattern from a book or magazine, fairly early on in the process I automatically think about what I can change and end up going off in a different direction. If you aren't familiar with this method, it may seem scary at first to deviate from written directions, but a charted pattern can be used as a springboard for your imagination.

One day I was showing these techniques to my dear friend and talented designer, Ellene Warren. We sat and knit lace together without any charts and she exclaimed, "I'm having so much fun, this is crazy! As a matter of fact, this is crazy lace!" And so it was named.

By combining the basic concepts of lace knitting with some ideas from the freeform fiber-arts world, Crazy Lace knitting offers a wonderful way to knit open, lacy fabrics in a new, inventive way. Once you understand a few simple rules of "lace logic", you'll be able to knit incredible, one-of-a-kind treasures that you never dreamed possible. It's an inspiring process!

With Crazy Lace, the possibilities for creativity are limitless. However, there are some good, simple suggestions I'll offer for a more enjoyable experience and successful outcome. Most importantly, what I hope I convey is to love what you're doing. Get lost in it, revel in it, find your rhythm and flow with it.

I encourage you to feel the freedom and joy that knitting lace creatively holds as you watch it unfold before your eyes. Knitting lace with this approach in mind is a blast, I promise. Go crazy and see what happens. Your adventure awaits!

thinking creatively and learning to let go

Here's the plan. Before we even get started, get a sturdy box with a lid. Not an actual box, but a box in your mind. Make it a lovely box, something you would use to store precious china or a spectacular hat. Start by filling that box with all the "I'm not creative", "I'm not an artist", "I can't", "That's ugly", "I'm not good enough" thoughts and any other negative feelings you can muster up at the moment. Don't worry about trying to fill it all at once; there's plenty of time and there will be plenty of other opportunities to add to it. Let's refer to it as "That Box".

Now, put a lid on That Box and take it to the attic of your imagination so that will be out of the way while you're knitting, but still easy enough to get to when another negative thought arises. I like to have my box close by for the inevitable "that's not very good" that sneaks in now and then. Don't hate the box. Just think of it as a container filled with items that are past their time and no longer useful. When a thought creeps back out of the box and pokes you in the side, as thoughts are prone to do, gently pick it up and return it to That Box.

OK, I think we're ready! Clearing your mind of the negative feedback loop we all carry around in our heads is a very important part of the creative process. What we're doing together in this book is more about creativity and self-discovery through knitting than about the knitting itself. Creativity is about allowing yourself not to be perfect. All of the preconceived ideas about what something's "supposed" to look like or doing it the "right way" go into the box and are forgotten for the moment. Sure, they'll sneak back in time, but it's good to keep them at bay as much as possible.

When it comes to knitting from patterns, there are lots of rules to follow to make sure a piece turns out as it was intended. The proper yarn and correct gauge are very important to ensure that something will fit properly. Pattern knitting is a wonderful thing, but a very different thing from creative knitting. One isn't better than the other and neither is right for everybody. Some people experience sheer joy in completing a pattern perfectly and find the creative process uncomfortable.

Crazy Lace doesn't have to mean knitting completely random, abstract patterns. We're not ignoring the world of lace charts and patterns by any means. There are many ways to incorporate familiar traditional charts and designs into creative knitting. There are times when I love knitting from patterns. I think it's important to continue to knit from patterns to learn as much as you can about the craft of knitting, but creative knitting is an entirely different mind-set that requires an open-minded approach. Allow yourself to be a little uncomfortable. It's the questions that lead us to new places.

I bow to the technically adept knitters who knit fine lace heirlooms. Their proficiency is awesome. There's no doubt that the more skillful you are, the better the outcome. However, I'm asking you to start with a clean slate. Enjoy the process before worrying about the results. This is not a license to knit sloppily. This is knitting with intention. When you work creatively you're watching what you're doing, following the journey rather than worrying about the final product. Don't fret about what anyone else will think about what you're creating.

It's hard to let go of the desire to be a perfect knitter, but for now allow yourself the freedom to breathe with your knitting and focus on the process. Just play. Discover yourself as you create. Enjoy the creative flow down your arms and out through your fingertips. Enjoy the pure pleasure of creating lovely, lacy fabric, right before your very eyes, with just two sticks and a string, the joy of asking what will happen if you just try something you may not have tried before. You'll fall in love with knitting all over again.

randomly symmetric
Rufflenutz™ scarf
various yarns
and needle sizes

a little lace background

Let me begin by saying I have the utmost respect for traditional lace knitting. I love knitted lace of any kind and stand in awe of the knitters who have, for centuries, produced breathtaking works. It was by learning, experimenting and modifying traditional lace styles that I developed these creative approaches. Everything in this book is adapted from the great traditions of lace knitting around the world.

Traditional lace knitting holds great intrigue and mystery with its deliberate, intricate structure forming delicate openwork. Works by the legends of lace knitting like Herbert Neibling make my head positively spin. It's amazing to see a knitted lace shawl and realize it's really just one long thread looped around and around itself to create such a magical fabric. Interestingly enough, as complicated as it looks, knitting lace is pretty simple once you understand the basic logic and have practiced some of the stitches and traditional patterns. Anyone who can cast on, bind off, knit, purl and yarn over can easily tackle lace knitting. The main stitches and techniques are created by variations of simple yarn-overs and corresponding decreases.

Lace knitting has been part of cultural traditions worldwide, passed along to new generations, as far north as the Arctic Circle. Orenburg lace from Russia, Shetland Lace and shawls from the Faroe Islands, Estonia and other parts of the world have lace traditions dating back centuries. If you're especially interested in the history of lace knitting I recommend reading Margaret Stove's *Creating Original Hand-knitted Lace*, which is a spectacular book and well worth locating.

In more modern times, lace knitting was revisited, researched and redesigned by great knitters like Mary Thomas and Elizabeth Zimmerman. After reading *Mary Thomas' Book of Knitting Patterns*, originally published in 1943, my mind was reeling with all kinds of ideas to incorporate into creative lace knitting. Mary Thomas presents simple medallion instructions that I've modified and adapted for the simple shapes in this book.

Elizabeth Zimmerman, EZ, is well known as the great pioneer who revolutionized the art of modern knitting. She is one of my knitting heroes. Her main message was to continue to experiment and develop your own style. She is well known for her Pi shawl, another wonderful building block for creative lace knitting.

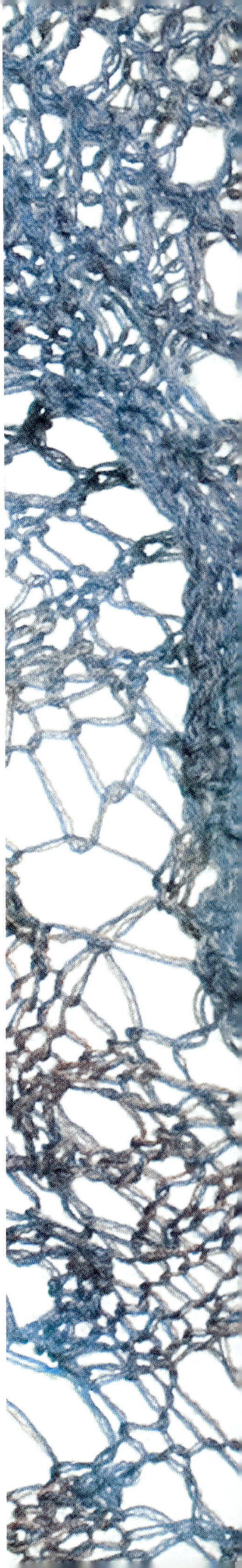

There are also wonderfully inspirational creative knitters who incorporate lace knitting into their work. One of my all-time favorite books is *Creative Knitting* by Mary Walker. Mary's approach to lace knitting is a thoroughly creative one. She explains different styles of knitting, how stitches are made, and presents her gorgeous wall hangings with instructions for the various stitches. Even though it's out of print and hard to find, it's worth buying if you run across a copy.

I also adore the modern Japanese stitch guides and lace pattern books currently available. If you'd like to collect a wide range of charts to incorporate into your lace knitting, check out books from Japan listed in the reference section. There are numerous knitting stitch dictionaries that include lace patterns and charts. I'll often sit with all my stitch guides spread out in front of me, modifying different instructions that strike my fancy as I knit.

There has been some controversy about the terms knitted lace versus lace knitting over the years. The difference is that "knitted lace" includes patterning on every other row while "lace knitting" refers to patterning done on every row. There are some lace knitters who still prefer to make a distinction between the two terms, but for the sake of creative lace, there's no need to make any separation between the techniques since you are free to use either method, or any combination of them, at any time you like. The functional difference between the two methods is this: by creating holes every other row (knitted lace), the pattern remains more distinct and the weave of the overall fabric will be tighter, whereas patterning on both sides (lace knitting) has a much more open and airy effect and makes the fabric almost twice as big. Whenever I refer to either term, I'm really referring to the entire style of openwork knitting.

upper: knitted lace
lower: lace knitting

randomly symmetric
swirl circle shawl
Yarn Place, *Gentle*, laceweight
overdyed with purple hair-dye
Size 7/4.5 mm needles

what makes it crazy?

The whole concept is wonderfully simple. You have complete freedom to decide what to do next with each stitch you knit, row after row. Every row is a new opportunity. Using charts or not, there are an infinite number of ways to knit lace with very little planning. It sounds crazy, but you can do whatever you want, whenever you want, with very little to no planning ahead.

Crazy Lace can be wild and woolly or as refined as any heirloom lace knitting you've ever seen. It incorporates many traditional knitted lace techniques but it isn't restricted to specific motifs or pattern repeats. The true adventure of Crazy Lace is not knowing where you'll end up when you begin, yet finding an unexpected treasure at the end. There are endless ways to combine familiar patterning and stitches in some areas, but you don't need to make all your decisions before you start. You can experiment and knit completely randomly the entire time, knit symmetrically the entire time, or combine both methods in the same piece. The wonderfully liberating part of this process is that once you've decided on one of the basic shapes in this book and follow the general rules for that shape, you're free to do whatever you want within each row.

Combinations of stockinette, garter, motifs, regular and abstract patterns can all be incorporated in the same piece. There are even ways to modify the basic shapes.

My ultimate goal is to get you to the point where you go wild doing uncharted, free-style lace knitting to your heart's content. Before we dive into the deep end it's important to understand how lace patterns work. To get you started we'll experiment with sampler style knitting, combining different charted lace designs. By beginning with various traditional stitches, you'll start to understand the structure of lace fabric and see how stitches work together. Once you're comfortable, we'll explore a completely random approach to Crazy Lace where no advance charting is necessary.

If you're already familiar with lace knitting, feel free to skip the sampler section and jump right into Crazy Lace. If you've never knit lace before, it's good to start with charted designs. Throughout this experimentation, hopefully you'll also discover a new way of looking at your knitting and find yourself considering adding different techniques to your general work too.

I'll guide you through my approach to creative lace knitting but you'll undoubtedly discover much more exploring on your own. I've limited the instructions in this book to classic, basic shapes for shawls and scarves, but any of these techniques can also be incorporated into other clothing or accessories as wearable art.

how to use this book

Making Crazy Lace is easy!

Part 1 includes an introduction to materials and complete instructions on how to create, modify and improvise lace patterning using Lace Logic™.

Part 2 contains directions on starting basic shapes, which are shown in stockinette stitch. With your knowledge from Part 1, you'll be ready to replace the stockinette areas with lace patterning of your choice and continue knitting until your piece is the desired size.

Part 3 explains how to add beautiful borders, embellishments and ruffles to your Crazy Creation.

The most important thing to remember is to relax, have fun and go a little crazy!

materials

part 1

yarn

weight and content

Traditional lace shawl and scarf patterns are usually worked in very fine, lace-weight yarns. Lace yarns are sometimes referred to as "gossamer" or "cobweb" depending on how many plies it has. Since you'll be knitting lace creatively, however, you're free to experiment with different yarns of all different weights and fibers to see what happens with each. Sock yarn and fingering weight yarns are wonderful for lace knitting but try even heavier weights of yarn with larger needles. Try combining different yarns within the same piece. Find several yarns of similar weight and color but very different texture and switch them as you knit to achieve a gorgeous effect. Most lace patterns show up best in smooth yarns, but there are lots of fun and funky fibers that work beautifully for lace knitting.

Since all lace knitting needs to be blocked to reveal the lace patterning, the fiber content is very important. The yarn you choose should provide a good amount of elasticity since it's going to be stretched quite a bit. Many yarns are intended to knit socks specifically and include a nylon content. If the percentage of nylon is over 15%, your lace will have a tendency to spring back to it's original knitted size and will need frequent re-blocking. Cotton and other plant-based fibers have less elasticity than wools but can be used when you want a stiffer, crisper final fabric for items like table linens or handbags. Silk works wonderfully when mixed with wool fibers but tends to be too limp and inflexible on its own. Synthetic yarns mixed with wool are nice and light-weight. The best way to determine if any yarn will work for a given project is to swatch out a section of lace about six inches square, approximating the technique you'll use, then block it to see how it drapes.

same stitch, different yarn and needles

same yarn, different needles

My favorite lace knitting yarns are: merinos, alpacas and of course, cashmere! Man-made materials can work if the fibers are soft enough. The time you invest in a lace project is usually substantial, so it's worth spending the extra money to use a yarn you love for the unique heirloom you're about to create. Most importantly when choosing any yarn - you've got to love it! Try a bunch to see what you like. If you're working with one that doesn't feel good, don't use it! If you don't like the yarn you won't enjoy the process. Using a yummy yarn that feels good slipping through your fingers makes a huge difference.

Another important factor to consider when choosing yarn is drape. Pick a yarn that's soft to the touch and feels good against your skin. Any yarn you choose will drape differently depending on the size needles you use. Try different sized needles with each yarn to decide what will give you the desired result. The same yarn knit on a pair of needles a couple sizes larger or smaller may look totally different after it's knitted and blocked like the samples to the right. Take some time and try a swatch to see the result before you commit to a larger project.

Also consider the final weight of the piece you want to make. For a larger shawl you might want to use larger needles and a lighter, loftier yarn like mohair to keep it from getting too heavy.

yarn amounts

Determining how much yarn you need for a specific piece can be done by looking at similarly sized lace patterns to determine their yardage. Crazy Lace uses approximately the same amount of yarn as any other lace knitting.

Checking an existing pattern that uses a similar gauge can give you a good estimate. The wonderful thing about shawls and scarves is that you can determine the desired size as you knit and allow them to grow as your yarn quantity permits. Basically, you can keep knitting until your yarn runs out! I usually estimate 300-400 yards of laceweight yarn on size 5/3.75mm- 7/4.5mm needles for a scarf, 400-600 yards for a stole and 800-1200 for a large shawl.

Most lace-weight yarns are sold with a much longer yardage than sock, sport or worsted weight yarns, sometimes as much as 600-900 yards per ball. Since you're making openwork fabric, lace-weight yarn has a tendency to go much farther as well. I've made a number of stoles from just one or two balls of lace-weight yarn! Heavier gauge yarns also give you more yardage when you knit lace since the fabric uses up less yarn than a piece made as a solid fabric. More holes = less yarn (but your yardage may vary). I normally like a smooth texture to lace yarns, since fluffier yarns like mohair generally don't show the stitches as well. However, when you work with larger than usual needles the fluffier yarn can yield exquisite results. Textured yarns may be difficult to rip out if you decide to frog a few rows while you're working.

Regardless of the type of yarn or content, it's very important to block a sample swatch to see the final results before you start on the major piece.

One more quick mention about any lace-weight yarn you choose: try to have as few joins in the yarn as possible. Even if they're tiny, knots or woven-in ends will show up after the lace has been blocked. I like to use a Russian join for connecting any new yarn.

laceweight

fingering weight

russian join

laceweight: Loop new yarn over the tail of the old yarn and twist gently.
Resume knitting.

fingering weight and heavier yarns: Loop new yarn over the tail of the old yarn. Baste a few stitches through the same yarn with each tail and pull tightly. Trim ends and resume knitting.

three different yarns in the same stitch pattern and same sized needles

color

Traditionally, lace was knit in light colors, but Crazy Lace can be made with absolutely any color. I like to use lighter or brighter colors since they show the lace patterning better than darker yarns. Color is a subjective matter, so the choice of a color can change the entire feel of a project. The same stitches knitted in a light color and a vibrant color will have a very different effect. Think about what you're creating and what mood you want to evoke. Choose colors that are pleasing to you and you know you'd enjoy wearing or gifting. You can choose one color for the entire piece or combine several colors by striping from one to the next.

Variegated yarns are gorgeous but are not always the best choice for lace. A heavily variegated yarn may obscure your stitch detail and confuse the lace patterning, which defeats the whole purpose of lace knitting. Even if it looks beautiful as a skein, yarn with variegation that has extreme color or value changes in short repeats will often look too splotchy when knit.

As with any yarn choice, experiment with a variegated yarn by trying it out first, knitting and blocking a swatch to see how you feel about it before embarking on a large project or investing in an expensive variegated yarn. Keep in mind that a small swatch will display color changes differently than a large piece, but it will give you some idea of how the yarn will look when knit.

solid and variegated yarn in the same stitch pattern and same sized needles

There are some wonderful yarns with very long color repeats that blend from one color to the next very slowly. These are gorgeous for lace knitting. I've listed a few favorites in the resource section. If you find a yarn that has a shorter color repeat with a very subtle color change you may be able to use it. I commonly use one color throughout an entire piece but there's no reason not to experiment with different colors in the same piece.

If you aren't happy with the color, you can very easily over-dye a piece after it's knitted. Wool yarn absorbs dye wonderfully. I've re-dyed several pieces after I completed them when I found the color wasn't what I wanted or the variegation was too distinct. Soak the piece in Rit™ color remover first, rinse well and re-dye it with a new color. You can also achieve a wonderful hand-painted look by allowing some sections to soak longer than others or by splattering different colors of dye over a finished piece.

above from lower left:
- glass circulars from glasspens.com
- Addi lace needles
- Knitpicks Harmony
- Knitpicks Options
- Signature stilleto tips
- ponyneedles.com
- Inox circular needles

needles

A pointy needle makes all the difference when it comes to enjoying knitting three, four or five stitches together. I like needles with the sharpest points possible. Most needles feel like you're knitting with butter-knives when you knit lace. It's worthwhile to invest in a separate set of needles with pointier tips. You might even end up using them for ALL your knitting like I do! I've listed some favorites in the reference section but try a number of needles to see which you prefer.

Different yarns react and move differently on different needle surfaces. Try wood, aluminum, brass and glass to see which "slip" the best but aren't too slippery with your choice of yarn. There are wonderful needles made especially for lace that have sharper points and a bit of a drag to the metal so the stitches don't pop off too easily. Lace stitches have a tendency to try to jump off some needles, especially metal ones, so just changing to wood can make a big difference in your knitting experience. You want to make sure you're as happy as possible with your needle and yarn combo so you're not fighting your stitches.

I prefer circular needles, but many knitters like straight needles. The choice is yours. The amazing thing about using lace-weight yarns is that literally hundreds of stitches can easily squish onto short, straight single or double-pointed needles. The most important thing to consider with circular needles is a good, clean join between the needle and the cable itself. Yarn-over stitches have a tendency to tighten up when they're resting on the cable. If the join is bumpy or uneven, you can end up with torn fibers and undue frustration from trying to slide the yarn-overs back onto the needles from the cable.

left:
randomly symmetrical
tip-to-top triangular shawl
Jojoland, *Harmony*
in color- HC03
Size 7/4.5 mm needles

needle size

The general rule of thumb for lace is to use needles at least two sizes larger than the recommended size on the ball band but if you want more stitch definition, you can use smaller needles. Larger needles not only make larger holes but they also make a thinner, drapier fabric. Try several sizes with the same yarn to see which you prefer. My favorite go-to needles are size 5, 6 and 7 when I'm working with lace-weight to fingering weight yarn but I'll go up to sizes 8-11 for a heavier or fuzzy yarn like mohair.

other tools

There really are very few other tools you need for knitting lace. It's good to collect all your tools first so you have them available when you need them.

Stitch markers are an integral part of lace knitting if you're creating specific patterns or specific sections. The markers help you easily keep track of pattern repeats or sections of knitting. Use the smallest, thinnest stitch markers you can find. Closed jump rings are wonderful if there are no sharp edges to catch on the yarn. There are lots of wonderful, decorative and fun stitch markers that are great to collect but are not what you want to use for lace knitting. Any dangly parts will snag your knitting, something you want to avoid at all cost.

A flexible measuring tape is handy for blocking to make sure the sides of a piece measure the same. We'll go into the specifics of blocking later.

A small pair of scissors and a crochet hook for casting on and binding off are also handy to have available. To make sure the cast-on and bound-off edges aren't too tight, I use a crochet hook that's at least a size larger than the needles I'm going to use. It's also handy to have a smaller crochet hook ready in case you drop a stitch.

While you are knitting, good lighting is essential. Pick a comfortable place to sit where you don't have to bend over or hunch your shoulders. No need to tense up - this should be fun and relaxing!

After your lace is finished, the final step is called blocking. An appropriate blocking surface is essential. There are lots of ways to go about blocking your pieces. Depending on whether you steam or wet block, you'll want to decide on a method and get the right tools for the best result. I prefer wet blocking, which requires a large water-proof surface, towels and rust-proof T-pins. If you want to steam block your piece with a good iron, make sure you have a wide, flat surface you can protect from the heavy blasts of steam, as well as rust-proof T-pins.

taking care of yourself

One more thing I want to address is knitting fatigue. Since a good deal of manipulation is done repeatedly to decrease stitches, you need to take regular breaks and relax your hands. The worst thing you can do is cause cramping and pain in your fingers, wrists and elbows from knitting. Having suffered a knitting injury that cost me a year of not being able to knit and months of physical therapy, I can attest to how important it is not to overdo it! I ignored the warning signs and worked while my hands ached, ending up with a pinched nerve in my neck from being way too tense. Not fun! Take a few minutes and stretch your fingers, make fists and relax them and do wrist circles to loosen up any tightness. Get up and walk around a bit, roll your head from one side to the other to loosen your neck, take deep breaths and relax your shoulders. Try to integrate some stretching and regular breaks into your knitting routine to preserve your body. This will allow you to continue to knit for longer periods of time. Most importantly, don't forget to breathe deeply and allow yourself to fully relax. It's easy to tense up and want to knit faster and faster so take some time, shake it out and enjoy the process.

lace logic

how lace is created

Holes in lace knitting are such a good thing that we make them intentionally! In very basic terms, increases are paired with decreases to create abstract or specific designs. The positions of the holes and decreases relative to each other create the patterning. Each stitch alone makes less of an impact on the overall design than the way the holes are placed in relationship to each other. Designs are created by moving the direction of the holes over rows spaced with areas of plain knitting.

The foundation of all lace is the eyelet stitch, a yarn-over increase paired with a decrease, usually by knitting two stitches together, [yo, k2tog]. There are a multitude of variations of how and when to do the increase and decrease that create different lace effects. For instance, you have the option of knitting two stitches together and adding a yarn-over increase before or after that decrease.

left: stockinett
right: garte

diagonal square baby blanket wit
random eyelet
Feza, *Alpine Ligl*
Size 5/3.5mm needle

However, not every yarn-over/decrease pair has to happen adjacent to each other in a row, or even in the same row. Decreases can be separated from the increases by a few stitches or happen right next to each other. We'll explore why this happens in some designs, how it affects the overall fabric, and when you would use one or the other approach.

How stitches are knit or purled makes a difference in how the patterning in the final fabric appears. There are many more choices than just knitting on one side and purling on the other (stockinette stitch), or knitting on both sides (garter stitch). Try combining eyelets with knit and purl stitches on both sides or use a specific stitch pattern like a seed or moss stitch for different effects. Experiment with knitting and purling through the back loops to create twisted stitches. The same patterns worked in garter and stockinette stitches have different appearances. Stockinette stitch fabric tends to show directional lines and ridges more than a garter base. Make a swatch of each with the same yarn to see how each looks. It's also good to know that garter stitch fabric has a tendency to expand or grow more lengthwise after blocking.

The number of holes in each row will change the fabric stability and the drape significantly. Adding more holes in a row creates a more open fabric, so increasing or decreasing the number of holes per row can alter the actual drape of the fabric.

scarf with random meandering
lines, nuppes and irregular borders
Curious Creek Fibers, *Wasonga*
Size 6/4mm needles

Holes on every other row create a tighter and sturdier fabric than holes knitted on both sides. Use both approaches as you like within the same piece to achieve different effects and create different fabrics.

The size of the holes will also affect the pattern of the lace motifs. Larger holes make a less recognizable, open design whereas tighter holes will preserve the stitch pattern. One is not preferable over the other and depending on the desired final affect, either can be used.

Textured stitches are less noticeable if the yarn is fine, although stitches such as brioche, bobbles or any other textured stitches can be incorporated to vary the surface and texture of the fabric as well. Try mixing in different types of stitches to see what happens. Use larger needles to achieve a lacy effect with any number of solid stitch patterns.

increases and decreases

Now that you know that lace is created by combining increases and decreases to create holes, you have a multitude of options for how you can combine those stitches. A base of garter stitch fabric doesn't show much difference in directional decreases but a stockinette base will show the slant of a decrease either left or right, which can be used for specific effects.

increases

The most common type of increase in lace knitting is done on the right side row between knit stitches and is called a yarn-over: taking the yarn to the front of the right needle and passing it up, over the top, to the back without knitting a stitch. On the next row, this stitch is worked like any other stitch and counts as a new stitch. Yarn-overs can be done between other types of stitches and from either side of the fabric as well. Other types of increases that might be used include knitting into the front and back of the same stitch, knitting into the bar between the stitches on the same row or picking up the stitch wrap from the previous row and knitting into it and then into the stitch itself. If you were knitting a garment following a pattern and combining lace into it, you may want to use the other types of increases to shape the fabric. However, these other types of increases don't make a hole, so most of the time you'll want to use a yarn-over as your increase for lace patterning. Doubling or tripling the yarn-overs in one row and releasing all but one on the next row can make even larger holes. The overall width of a piece can increase at any time by casting on more stitches.

creating different sized stitches and holes

It's really fun to watch the lace fabric grow as you knit and follow the lines and patterns that develop. Another interesting way to vary the overall fabric and pattern is by changing the hole sizes from one row to the next.

My most favorite technique is to knit into a hole two or three rows below. A compensating decrease can be done either by dropping the stitch directly above it or decreasing somewhere in the same row to compensate for the added stitch. Knit into a hole one or two rows below, knit one, then knit back into the same hole again to open it up even more. Remember to decrease accordingly. If there's a yarn-over above a hole on a previous row, drop the yarn-over and knit into the hole to count as one stitch. A lace-weight yarn generally works best for this technique but experiment with heavier yarns, too. Slip stitches from one row to the next for a row or two without knitting them to elongate a stitch. Remember that

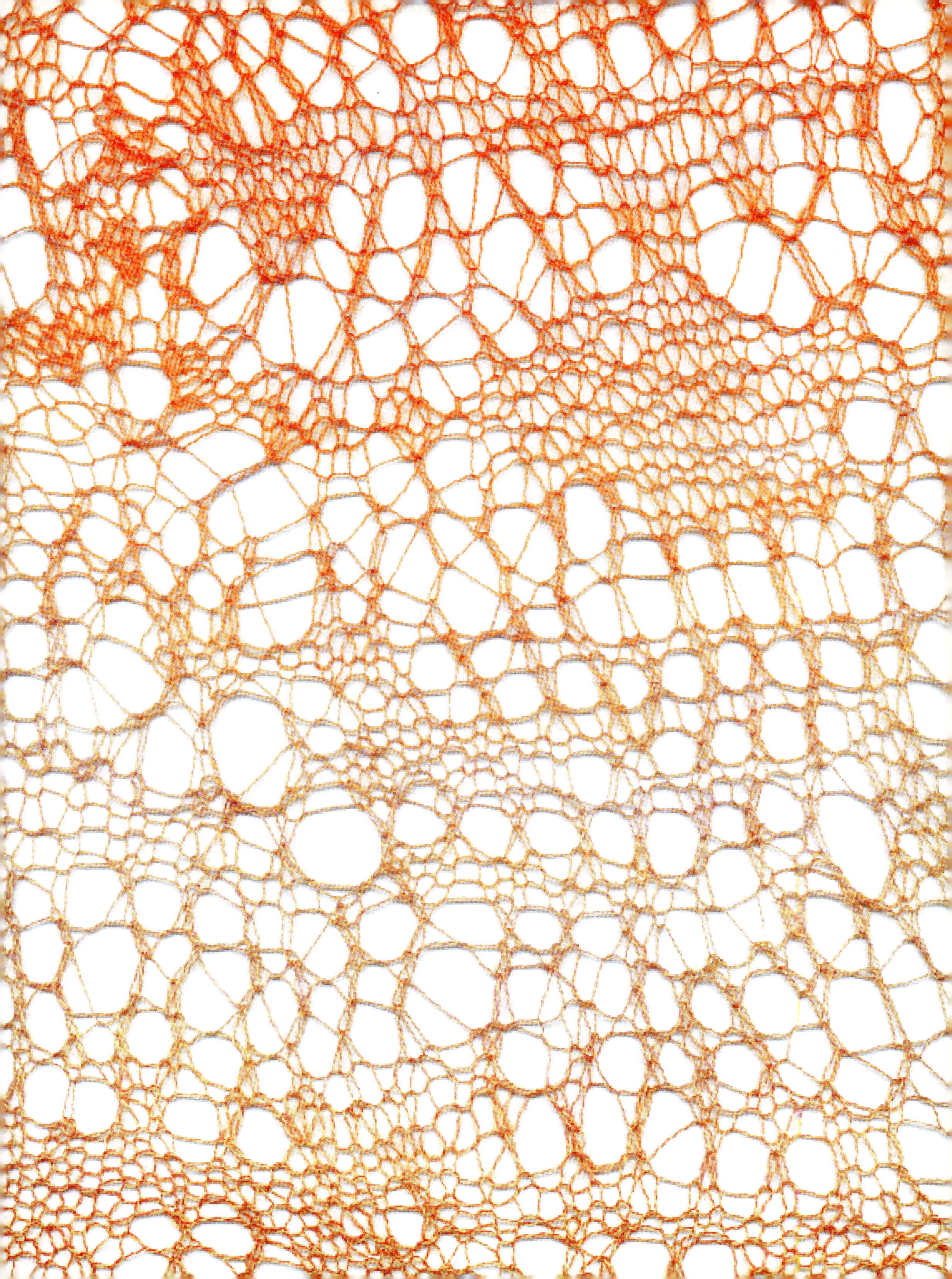

knitting through the back loop has a different effect than knitting through the front loop and combining knitting and purling on the same row will also vary the surface texture.

Change needle sizes to create a whole row or area with larger holes. This will also expand the width without increasing the stitch count. By going up a needle size every few rows you can also increase the shape of the overall piece. Using larger or smaller needles is a great way to vary the size of the holes but be aware that the entire shape changes as well.

common increases

yo: yarn over one or more times
M1: make one by lifting the bar between stitches
kfb: knit into front and back of the same stitch one or more times
kyok: knit, yarn over, knit in same stitch one or more times
M1below: make one stitch by knitting into the stitch or hole in a previous row
M1-r: make one by lifting the bar around the stitch to the right
M1-l: make one by lifting the stitch below the next stitch you are about to knit
(Any of these can be done with purl variations as well)

decreases and directional stitches

Decreases are a little more complicated. Decreases reduce the stitch count by combining two or more stitches into one stitch. There are numerous ways to do decreases, including knitting or purling two stitches together, slipping a stitch, knitting or purling the next stitch and passing the slipped stitch over and off the needle, or binding off, along with a number of other methods all listed below. The reason there are so many variations in decreasing is that the way a decrease is done makes it slant either to the left or the right or to remain centered. You can use the directional decrease to create lines of ridges that run through your fabric, making abstract or specific patterns, or decrease so that it leaves no ridge at all.

Lace-weight yarns generally don't show the direction of the decreases as much as thicker yarns. Some lace knitters only use one method for all their decreases even when knitting a stockinette base with very fine yarn. Using heavier (fingering, sport or worsted weight) yarns, knitting stockinette or knitting a tighter weave in the fabric makes the decrease ridge become more noticeable.

Single decreases, reducing two stitches to one stitch, are commonly paired with a yarn-over by knitting two stitches together to create a right-leaning slant (abbreviated as k2tog).

To create a left-leaning slant, slip a stitch to the right needle, knit the next stitch and pass the slipped stitch over the knit stitch and off the needle (skp). Another method for creating a left-slanting decrease is to slip two stitches to the right needle knitwise one at a time, then knit them together (ssk).

Double decreases, decreasing three stitches to one, can be done several ways. One method is to simply knit or purl three stitches together, producing a right-leaning decrease (k3tog or p3tog). Another method is to slip one stitch knitwise, knit the next two stitches together, then pass the slipped stitch over the remaining knit stitch (sk2p). This is a left-leaning decrease. By slipping two and knitting one, then passing the two slipped stitches over a centered decrease occurs.

common decreases

centered:

sk2p: Slip 1 knitwise, knit 2 together, pass slipped stitch over
s2kp: Slip 2, knit 1, pass both slipped stitches over

right leaning:

k2tog: knit 2 stitches together
k3tog, k4 tog: knit the specified amount of stitches together

left leaning:

k2tbl: knit 2 together through back loop
p2tog: purl 2 together
p3tog, p4tog: purl the specified amount of stitches together
ssk: slip the first st knitwise, sl the next st purlwise, insert left needle through the back loop of both stitches and knit together
skp: slip one, knit one, pass slipped stitch over
sk2p: slip one stitch as if to knit, knit 2 together and pass the slipped stitch over

creating lace patterning

Pairing increases and decreases in different ways creates a multitude of options in the overall patterning of lace designs. Along with the holes, sharp lines are created when the pairs are kept adjacent. A curvier wave is achieved when the yarn-overs are separated from the decreases by several stitches. The larger the separation, the curvier that section will be. This also influences the edges of the fabric. When yarn-overs and decreases are separated, the bottom and top edges of the fabric tend to curve and ripple accordingly, as in a traditional lace pattern like Feather and Fan. This change of shape happens because several decreases next to each other draw the fabric in and several increases next to each other expand that section of the knitting out.

Lines and ridges can travel through the fabric in specific directions along with the holes. Decreasing before or after the yarn-over and the direction the decrease slants will also make the ridge more or less apparent. Continuing to knit across all the stitches in the row for a few rows and then the changing direction of the decreases can also soften curves while still maintaining an apparent ridge, even if the yarn-overs are right next to the decreases.

By understanding directional decreases from one row to the next, you can achieve different effects deliberately. You can follow a chart to create a specific pattern or watch the lines and directions of the holes and ridges as you progress to each new row. You can create abstract designs by deciding while you knit each row in which direction you want to continue the patterning.

chart-your-own rectangular shawl
with separate, sewn-on borders
Claudia Hand Painted Yarn,
Fingering in Rubies Playing
Size 5/3.75mm needles

creating lace fabric

With any approach to lace, remember that for a shape to remain geometric, you need to maintain an even stitch count from row to row for the shape you're creating. For an abstract shape, the count can vary from row to row; different shapes can be created randomly as you knit by increasing and decreasing as desired. As with any knitting, the more decreases there are, the narrower the fabric will be, and the more increases, the wider it will be if there are no compensating stitches. For a completely abstract shape, like the example on page 66, it's best to vary the actual shaping of the fabric on the beginning and ends of the row rather than in the middle, since adding or subtracting more stitches within the row tends to "bubble" the fabric.

Increasing or decreasing at the sides creates variations in shapes without distorting the overall flatness of the lace fabric when it's complete. That said, not all lace stitch patterns maintain the same number of stitches throughout a row repeat. Some lace patterns are made up over a series of rows, starting with a specific number of stitches and ending with that same number of stitches before the next repeat. The number of stitches in the pattern may change within those rows but will return to the original count.

In the case of a square or rectangle, the stitch count will be the same from one row to the next to keep the width even. For other geometric shapes to grow, the fabric expands by increasing at regular intervals without a compensating decrease. Shapes can be worked from one end to the other, from the center out or from the outside in. Keep in mind that knitted lace grows about 25%- 30% or more when blocked. While knitting, lace has a tendency to scrunch up, disguising the real pattern until after it's blocked. The more holes that are included, the more the piece will expand. A piece with increases and decreases on every row can grow as much as 50%. If you want your finished piece to be a specific size, do a six-inch gauge swatch with whatever yarn and needles you want to use, approximating the style of lace you want.

Block the swatch to see how much it will grow. Unless you are making a garment, it's not important to get an exact gauge before starting. It is good, however, to have an idea of how the shawl or scarf will grow after it has been stretched and blocked so that it doesn't become "the scarf that ate a village" once it's done. Changing the needle size will also create a different weave so try different sized needles with the same yarn and see how that changes the effect of the overall patterns. Keep in mind is that including larger areas of stockinette between the holes will keep a specific pattern more defined. The more holes there are, the less obvious the overall lace design will be.

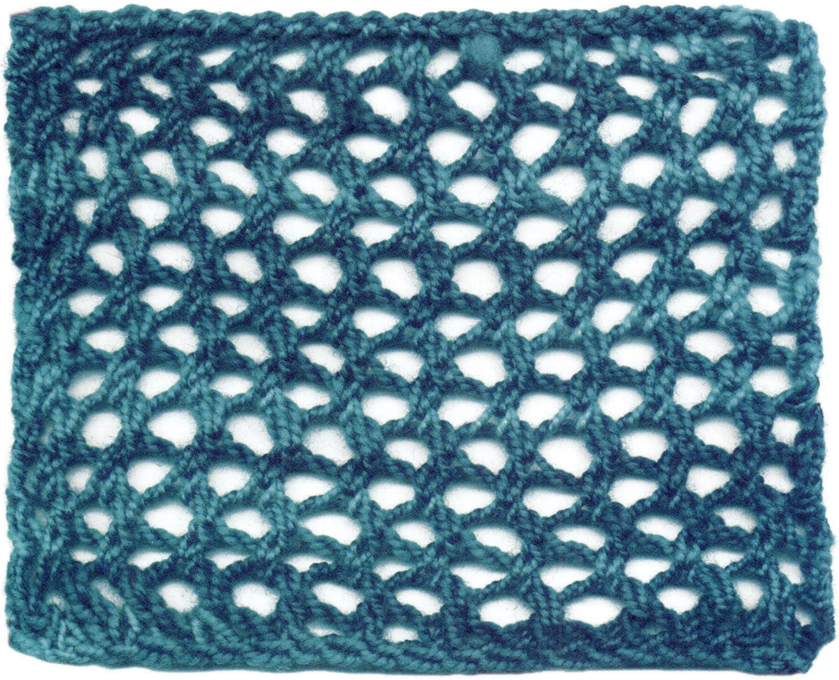

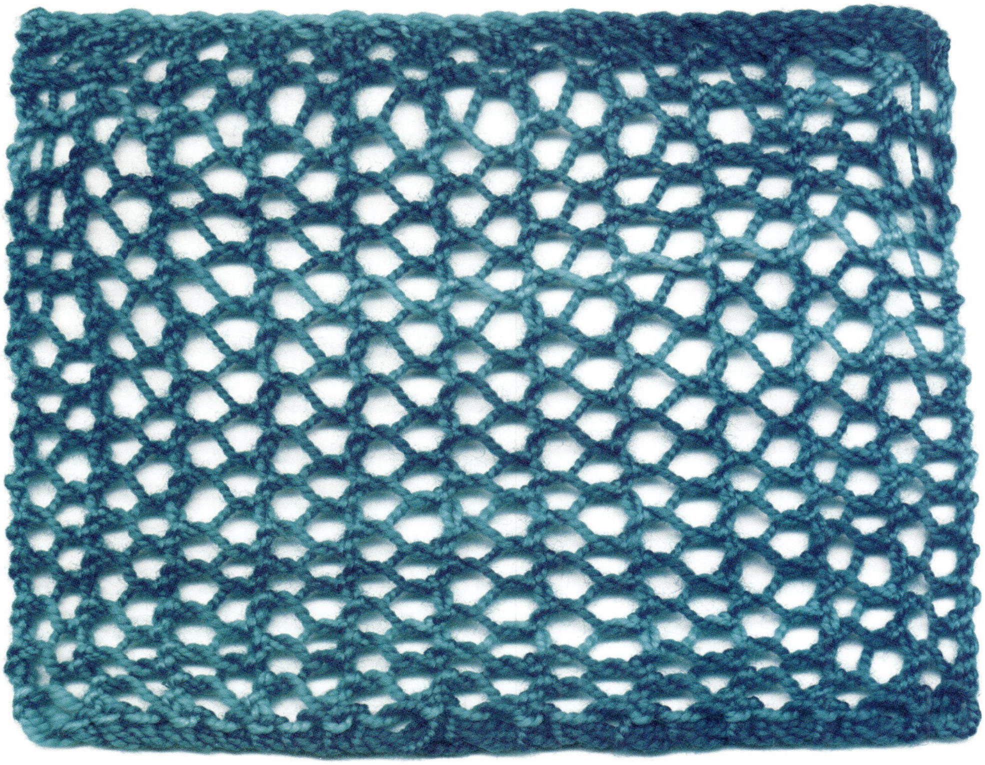

The three samples on this page were knitted with the same size needles and yarn.

The same stitch count of 30 stitches cast on and 30 rows completed was used for each swatch.

The top is stockinette stitch, the middle is knitted lace and the bottom is lace knitting.

The amount of lace patterning affects the finished size of any piece when blocked.

casting on and binding off

How you start and finish a piece of lace is just as important as how it is knit. An otherwise lovely shawl can be ruined by a cast-on edge that pulls in and can't be blocked to match the tension of the fabric. Since lace tends to grow widthwise as well as lengthwise, even if the cast-on is loose it will have a tendency to draw in with a regular cast-on edge. I find the best way to make sure the bottom edge isn't too tight is to do a crocheted provisional cast-on or crocheted cast-on and bind-off so the top and bottom edges aren't too tight. My general rule of thumb is to use a provisional cast-on for more than 10 stitches. I'll unzip the waste yarn, replace each live stitch onto a needle and bind those stitches off with a very loose crochet bind-off once the piece is complete. I'll even block the piece first before binding-off by threading a piece of waste yarn through the live loops before returning those stitches to the needle. When I finish the edge this way with a crochet bind-off I can be sure it's not going to be too tight. This is especially helpful with lace-weight yarn.

For a smaller amount of stitches, as in a circular shawl, use any cast-on you like. If you decide on another cast-on or bind-off, make sure to do it very loosely. You can do this by using needles two sizes larger than your working needles for the cast-on and bind-off.

The side edges of a piece of flat knitted lace are visible unless a border is attached later. To make sure the edges will be as attractive as possible, slip the first or last stitch on each row to create a finished edge that looks like a crocheted chain. Either slip the last stitch purlwise with yarn in front, turn the work and knit the first slipped stitch through the back loop, or slip the first stitch purlwise on every row. This slipped stitch at the beginning or end of a row is a good habit to get into even if a border will be attached later. The slipped stitches make it easy to see and pick up stitches evenly along the edges. Because some lace-weight yarns on larger needles leave too loose a chain at the edge with this method, it may not be necessary to do anything special at the beginning or end of a row when using a thinner yarn.

Knitting a few stitches on both sides at the beginning and end of each row before starting any patterning will create a garter stitch border. Stockinette edges will roll to the purl side if knit to the very end without a selvedge. Garter stitch edges will lie flatter and give the patterning a nice border. This type of edging isn't necessary if a border will be attached later since the border will help keep the edges flat.

Begin with a slip knot on the crochet hook and the knitting needle placed over the working yarn.

Reach over the needle with the hook, yarn over and pull a loop through the loop on the crochet hook.

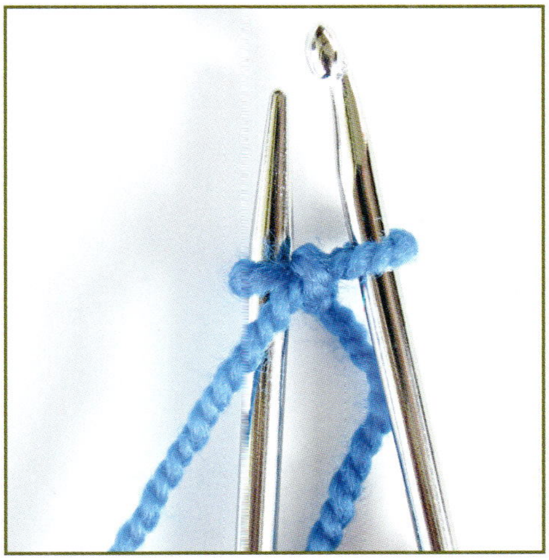

The working yarn is now in front of the knitting needle with one stitch on the needle and one on the hook.

Place the working yarn behind the needle to position it for the next stitch.

Continue the process of reaching across the needle and pulling through a loop for each stitch required.

The yarn ends up on top after each new stitch is made. Don't forget to return the working yarn to the back before starting the next stitch.

For a crochet cast-on, place the last stitch on the hook onto the needle. Count this as the last stitch.

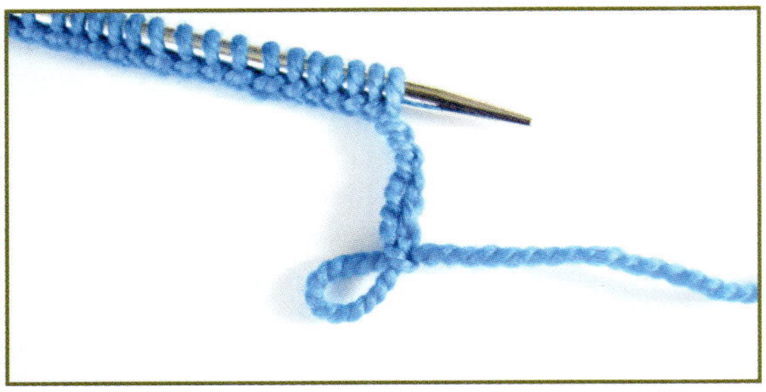

For a provisional cast-on, start with waste yarn and chain several past the last stitch. Secure the last loop with a safety pin or pull through gently. Begin the next row with main yarn.

crochet bind-off

There are numerous ways to bind off with a crochet hook to give the edge a finished look and keep it flexible. The method shown on this page uses a crochet slip stitch but it can also be done with a single crochet or even with one or more chains between stitches if more flexibility is needed.

Move the first stitch purlwise to a crochet hook. Insert hook into next stitch and yarn over.

Pull a loop through that stitch and the one on the hook.

Continue in this manner, inserting the hook knitwise into each stitch and pulling one loop through both stitches.

Make sure to size each stitch evenly as you pull a new stitch through.

Lengthen the new loop or add a chain between stitches to avoid pulling the edge too tight.

picot bind-off

Chain 3 to start the picot.

Slip stitch into the first chain made.

Continue to bind off with a slip stitch between each picot.

charts can be fun!

Mary Thomas was a pioneer of charted lace knitting in the 1930s. She believed that a good chart was all that is needed for lace instructions. Unlike written-out instructions, a chart actually shows what the lace will look like when it's complete. Once you learn this visual approach of "reading" a lace chart, you'll find it is much easier than trying to keep track of where you are in a written pattern. One of the best reasons to learn to read charts is that you can then use lace charts from all over the world without understanding the language. There are incredible charts from Europe and Asia that will make perfect sense once you see the logic of how they are drawn.

Lace charts are based on a simple grid system. The chart shows the pattern as it will appear on the right side of the fabric. Charts are read the same way you knit, from bottom to top, row by row. Right-side rows are read from right to left. Charts that are written for flat knitting are written so that wrong side rows are read from left to right. Numbers for each row are indicated next to the beginning of the row. Circular charts, like the ones for socks, are read from right to left on every round, since knitting in the round means that the right side is facing you at all times. Some charts, like the one below or at the end of this book, only show the pattern rows on the right side if the wrong sides are all knit or all purl. It's important to check the information in the beginning of each stitch guide or book to see how the charts are set up.

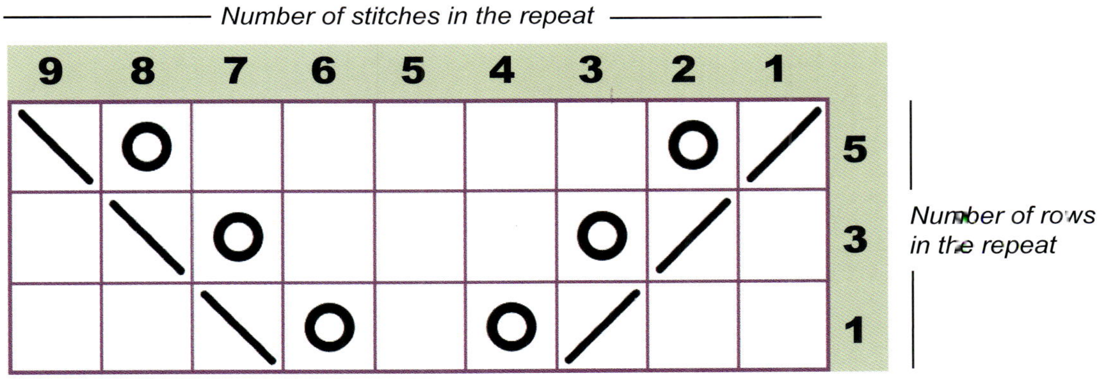

Patterns are created by repeating the same stitch instructions across the row in a specific multiple that equals the final stitch count for the row. Some patterns are very simple and are repeated over a few stitches, while others repeat over many stitches and a number of rows. Most lace charts are repeated evenly across a row and the multiple is completed at the end of the row, but since this is Crazy Lace, toss that idea into That Box we talked about earlier.

Each square on a chart contains a symbol which is an instruction. The symbols themselves are usually a visual representation of the stitch to be done; a yarn-over is an open O, a k2tog is a line that slants to the right.

Lace charts include a legend that defines each symbol. Most legends use symbols that are fairly universal but for a number of reasons, including limited printing space, some charts have their own symbols. Take a look at each chart legend to familiarize yourself with the symbols used in that particular pattern. Once you get used to reading charts you'll recognize the symbols easily.

For decreases, the direction of the slant of the symbol is the direction of the slant of the decrease. Any method you want to use to achieve the desired direction is perfectly fine as long as it's facing the same way.

If you are new to chart reading this bears repeating: charts are read from bottom to top.

legend

- k: knit
- p: purl
- yo: yarn-over
- k2tog: knit 2 together
- ssk: slip the first st knitwise, sl the next st purlwise, knit both slipped sts tog
- sk2p: slip1knitwise, k2tog pass slip stitch over
- k3tog: knit 3 together

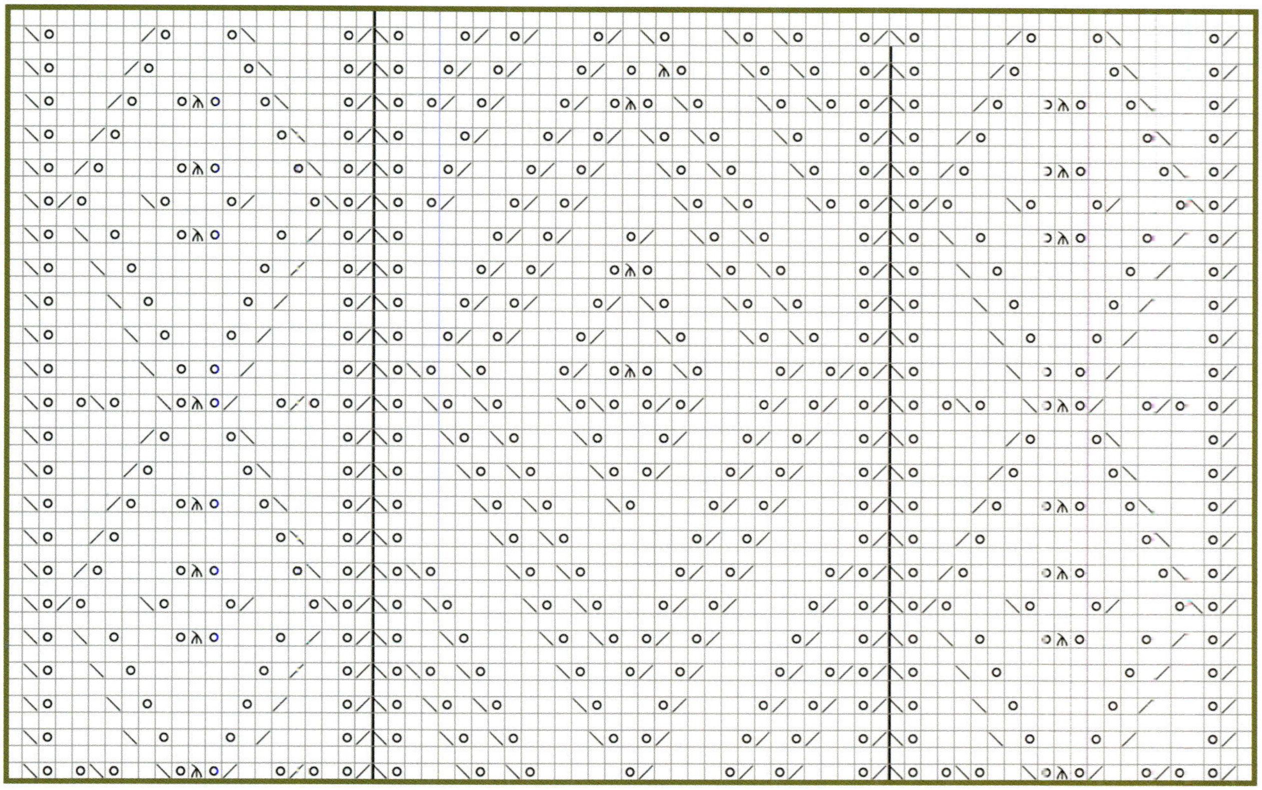

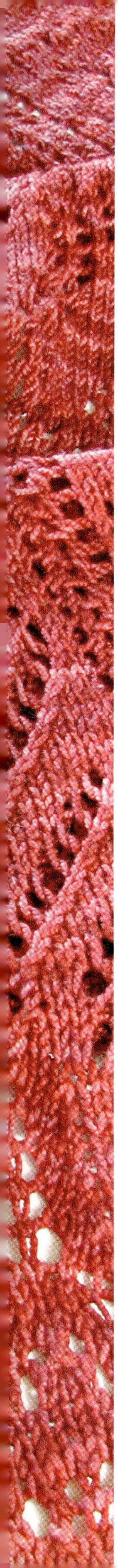

I like to use sticky notes or low tack adhesive tape to isolate the line of the chart I'm working on. I place it above the line I'm working on and move it up as I complete each row. A magnetic board and ruler or a stand from a stationary store are also useful to keep track of your place. When I find a chart I want to use in a book, I make an enlarged copy of the chart to follow rather than trying to read it out of the book.

Lace charts are usually accompanied by information indicating the number of stitches in a repeat and any other stitches that will be done at the beginning and/or the end of a row. The chart will show a section within the grid delineating the repeated stitches, with the extra stitches at the beginning and/or end of each row. For example, a chart that reads "multiple of 6 + 2" means that six stitches form the lace pattern repeat and the row may begin and end with one additional stitch on each side. In this case, the chart would show a grid with one dark vertical line after the first stitch, six boxes including symbols for the repeat, a dark vertical line for the end of the repeat and one final box for the last stitch in the row.

Sometimes the additional stitches are not evenly divided on either side of the repeated stitches, but are found only at the beginning or only at the end of the row, or unevenly spaced on either side. The number of stitches you cast on is any number that is a multiple of the stitch repeat plus the extra stitches if any are indcated. When the stitch multiple information is given, the additional number after the plus sign is only counted once in the total cast-on number.

+1	6	5	4	3	2	1	+1	
		O	⋀	O				7
			O	\				5
		O	⋀	O				3
	O		⋀		O			1

For example, if the multiple is 6 + 2 and you want the pattern to repeat five times across a fabric, you would cast on 32 stitches, 30 for the repeat (a multiple of 6) plus 2 for the extra, balancing stitches.

A stitch marker between each multiple helps keep track of your repeats as you knit across a row. Most lace patterns involve a few rows so each line above the one you're working on indicates the next line of knitting. Instead of thinking of each box as a stitch, read the boxes as you go across the row as an instruction for what to do next. One box may indicate knitting three stitches together and the box before and after it may indicate a yarn-over.

The total number of stitches will add up to three but the way to read it logically is to just do what it says next by the symbol indicated in the

boxes as you come to them rather than thinking of each box as an individual stitch.

For example, the chart to the right shows a k2tog followed by a yarn-over. The yo adds one stitch but the k2tog decrease restores the original count. The box with the k2tog indicates a direction regarding two stitches rather than just one stitch.

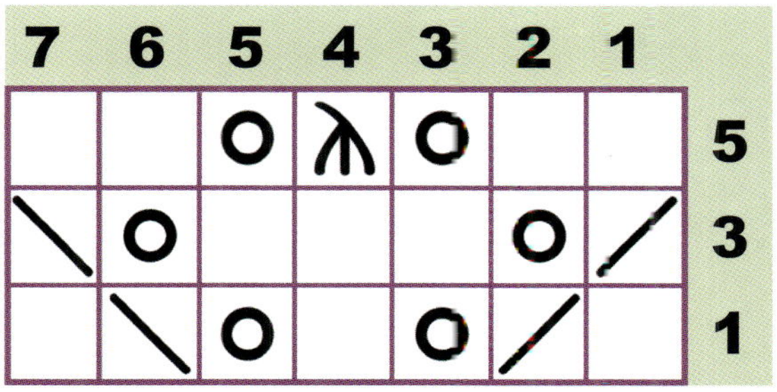

One of the things I love most about knitting lace is the rhythm. Keep your eye on the charts as you work. Eventually you'll start to see the patterns and find a rhythm in the repeats so that you don't need to refer to them as often. You don't need to memorize each line of each pattern repeat if you can easily follow along on a chart. It becomes second nature and you'll find your fingers dancing along when you repeat the pattern in your head - very meditative!

Don't worry about making mistakes. I'm giving you complete permission not to be perfect! If you make a mistake, rather than ripping out, continue on and notice how the pattern changes by skipping a stitch or adding an extra one somewhere. Although it feels scary at first, allow mistakes to happen and keep moving. It's an opportunity to learn something new and won't matter in the overall result since you're not trying to reproduce a specific pattern.

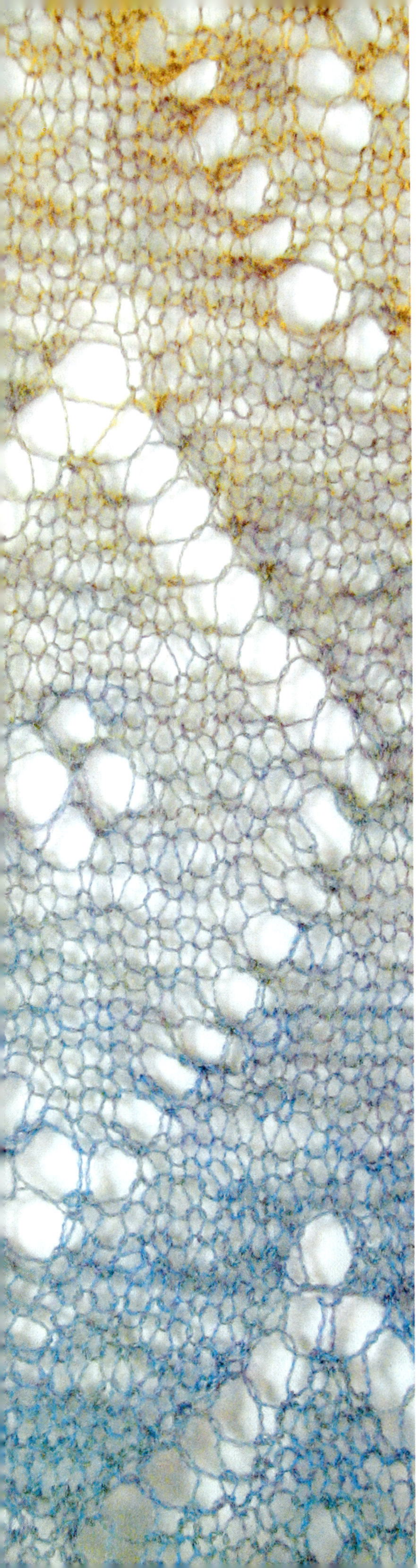

charting your own patterns

Charting patterns as you knit is a perfect way to keep a pattern symmetrical but still approach lace knitting creatively. Some knitters are uncomfortable with the thought that nothing is preplanned. Charts can easily be made for stitch repeats or whole areas of fabric when desired. The total stitch count can be divided into multiples or treated as one large area. It's easiest to place all of the yos on the chart first and then add compensating decreases once the patterning of holes is established.

I use a software program, Knit Visualizer, to chart my stitch patterns. You can experiment with this process using a photocopy of the knitting graph paper on page 99. If you find you enjoy charting your own Crazy Lace, I recommend buying the program. The website is listed in the resources section.

getting started

An easy way to embark on this Crazy Lace journey is to create a rectangular, stockinette sampler that includes different charted lace patterns and stitches. Stitch guides and lace knitting books are filled with gorgeous lace patterns. Many of them include easy-to-read charts. I'm including a number of stitch patterns starting on page 92, but you can also choose stitch patterns from other stitch guides.

Count the number of stitches on your needle minus two on each end for a selvedge. Divide the total by the stitch repeat you want to use to see if you need to add or subtract any more stitches before you begin the desired pattern. It's always nice to find lace patterns that use the exact multiples that divide evenly into the total stitch count on your needles, but sometimes you need to subtract or add a few stitches. Do this by separating one pattern from the next with a few rows of garter stitch, increasing or decreasing a few stitches within the garter stitch rows to compensate for the new multiple. After completing that section, increase or decrease to the count required for the next section.

Try to limit the increase or decrease to no more than two stitches so that the rectangle will maintain its shape. Although lace is very forgiving and can be blocked later to even out the edges, maintaining a consistent or nearly consistent stitch count is necessary to preserve a geometric shape.

a note about the stitch markers

It's easier to spot a mistake from one row to the next if you separate each repeat with markers. Markers allow you to see where you went wrong. Whether you rip back or not is up to you. Short repeats of three or four stitches do not need markers, but do continue to count "in your head" as you knit to check that the stitch count across the row remains the same. If you need to add or subtract stitches for a new design with a different multiple in the repeat, replace the markers to indicate the new multiple. Check your count before moving on to the next row to make sure the total stitch count is correct. I usually count along as I knit to keep track of the number of stitches in each repeat.

creating a sampler scarf

• Pick at least five stitch patterns to combine. Choose from patterns in this book or any other source, as long as the patterns contain the same multiple and are patterned only on one side. The included charts are all designed for flat knitting with the holes on every other row and show odd-numbered (right side) rows only.

• Before starting the main piece, begin with a crochet cast-on, knit a gauge swatch approximately six inches square, using one of your chosen patterns. Move the last row of stitches to a piece of waste yarn (do not bind off) and block your swatch. If you wish, knit another swatch with a different sized needle.

• Once you're comfortable with your choice of needles determine your gauge (number of stitches per inch). Multiply this number by the number of inches required for the desired width of the scarf. Divide this number by the number of stitches in your pattern repeat. If necessary adjust this number to an even number of repeats, and add four stitches (2 for the selvedge on each edge). Crochet cast on this number of stitches. (See page 41)

• Knit several rows of garter stitch before you start the first lace pattern.

• Before beginning the first chart, knit 2 stitches for the selvedge, place a stitch marker (PM), complete one multiple, PM, then continue across the row, PM between each repeat. PM before the last 2 stitches to remind you that these are selvedge stitches. (Always knitted on right and wrong side at the beginning and end of every row).

• Knit a few full repeats of the chosen pattern until you want to change the design. You can either knit a row or two of garter stitch between pattern changes or flow into the next pattern if the multiple stays the same.

• Continue to knit several full repeats of each pattern for as many rows as desired. Repeat the same patterns randomly to make the scarf longer or pick new designs to incorporate at any time.

You might decide to do half the scarf as a sampler and the other half with one specific lace pattern. It's totally up to you. Scarves are generally 64 to 72 inches long after blocking. Once you've knit about 45-50 inches bind off. Remember that blocked lace increases in length as well as width so block to desired measurement.

symmetrically patterned
sampler shawl
lace weight wool yarn
Size 4 needles

completely random
rectangular stole
with irregular borders
Yarn Place, *Gentle in Marooned*
Size 6/4mm needles

let's go crazy!

Now that you feel comfortable with the basic concepts of how lace patterns and stitches are created and work together, you're ready for the next step: Crazy Lace! This style of knitting lace is approached in an entirely different manner than traditionally charted lace. In this chapter you'll learn two different approaches: symmetrical and random. In both cases, you are free to experiment with making holes however you'd like, deciding where and when to direct specific patterns as the piece is knitted. Your final piece can be either style or a combination of both.

symmetrical crazy lace

There are several ways to create symmetrical patterning in Crazy Lace. One way is to follow the rules of multiples to create repeats by dividing the total stitch count into equal amounts. Decide on any sequence that will fit into that multiple and repeat it across the entire row evenly. Symmetry is easily maintained by changing the sequence as desired from one row to the next. Use familiar lace patterns or just wing it and make up a new sequence every single row. Chart out the repeat over a few rows, if you'd like, to design a specific pattern. Have fun combining patterns you're already familiar with while making new up ones.

When you want to change to a new pattern, start with a new multiple that's divisible into the final stitch count or use a new stitch pattern with the same multiple. A row or two of eyelet, garter or stockinette stitch is a nice way to delineate sections of new patterns. If you prefer, run one lace pattern right into the next without any separation.

Another approach is to make up each row as you knit. Repeat a sequence as if it were a charted repeat without deciding beforehand what that repeat will be. Remember, every row is a new opportunity! With this technique, you can improvise and maintain a symmetrical appearance. There are different ways of continuing the same stitch pattern over a number of rows when a shape increases regularly, like a triangular shawl. One way is to isolate the area of increase after each section marker with a second marker.

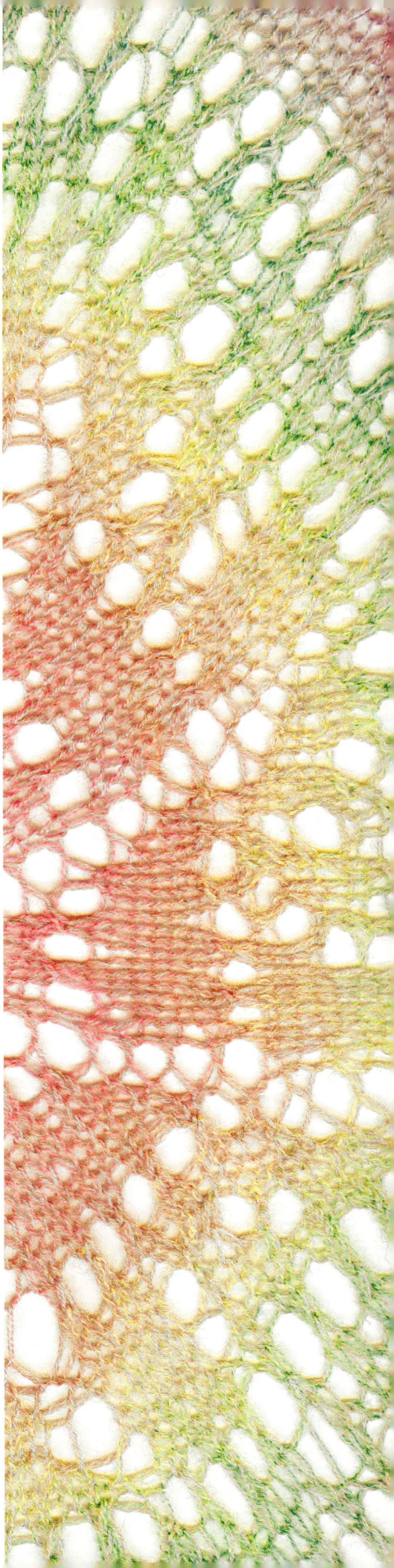

Continue the increases separately from the overall stitch pattern, only increasing between the original and new markers and not in the main area of each section. By isolating the main stitches, the specific pattern will always begin and end with the same number of stitches and be easy to keep track of from one row to the next and all of the increases are separated by the markers between the sections without having to incorporate them into the stitch pattern. Create alternate patterning in the separate area of growing increases. This method creates new wedges between each section of established stitch pattern.

A different approach is to incorporate a new repeat into the shaping when enough stitches are increased to the necessary multiple. This method continues the same pattern with a smoother transition and little to no interruption. For instance, a five stitch pattern repeat can be worked in an increase section after five stitches have been added. While the increases are being made, any combination of stitches can be formed to simulate that pattern but it does not have to be the exact pattern repeat until you have enough stitches to start another full repeat. In this case, place a marker between each full section and the increases until enough increases have been made. The increase marker is then moved to include the additional repeat in the main section and a new increase section begins. This method creates a more continuous flow from one area to the next and maintain the same pattern.

Many pattern repeats can easily be altered for different multiples by adding stitches before, after or within the repeat itself.

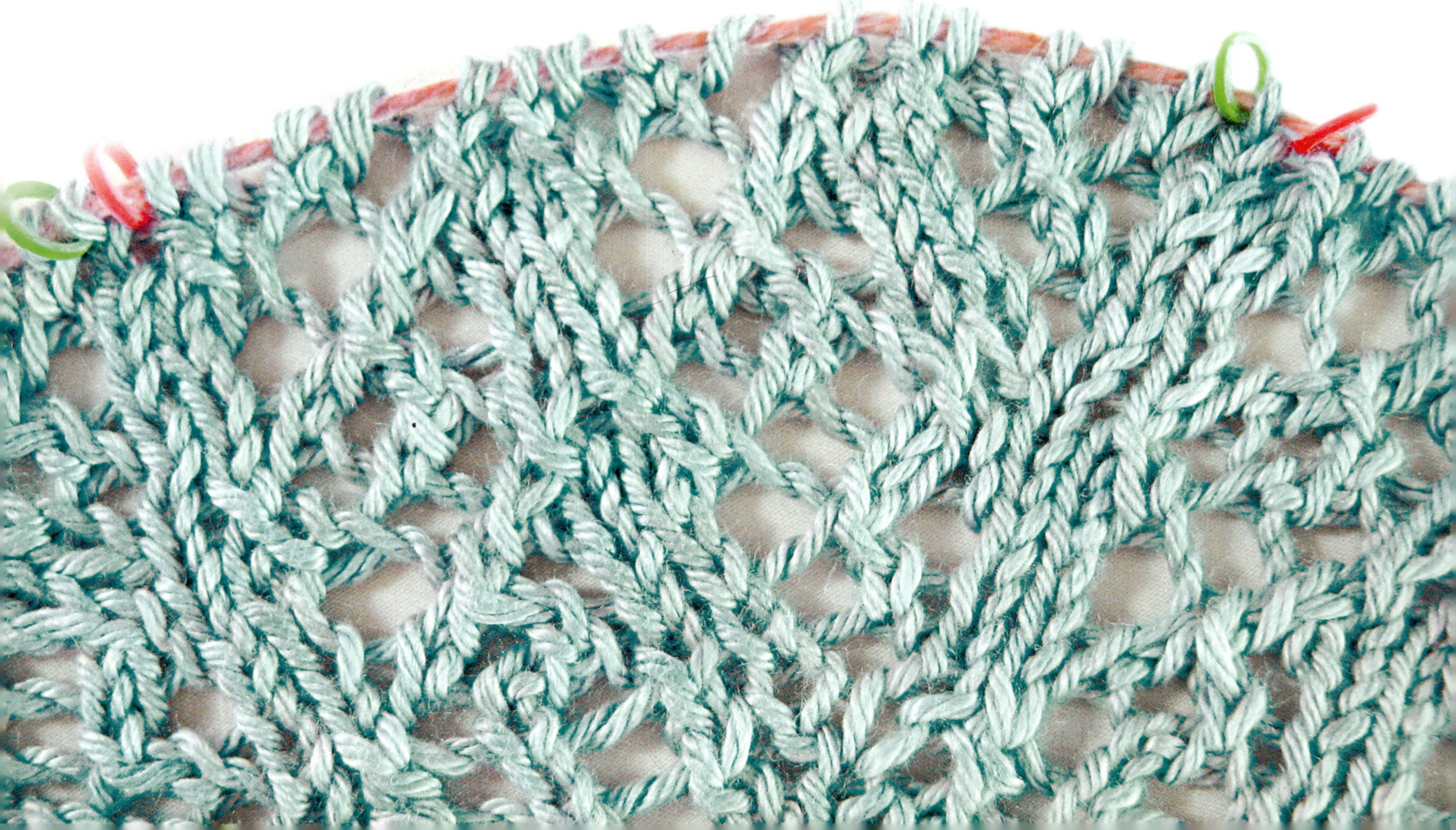

symmetrically patterned
semi-circle shawl with
separate increase sections
Claudia Hand Painted Yarn
Fingering in Tranquility
Size 5/3.75mm needles

An additional knit stitch, an area of ribbing between stitches or any other stitch can be added to an existing pattern and recharted into a multiple that equals the appropriate stitch count. The chart below shows a seven stitch repeat changed to an eight stitch repeat two different ways. The second chart shows a knit stitch added in position 8. The third chart shows the additional stitch added in position 5 and the sk2p changed to k2tog, ssk in row 5.

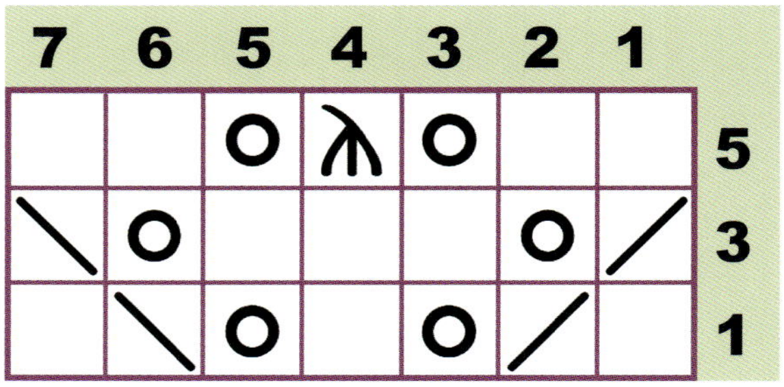

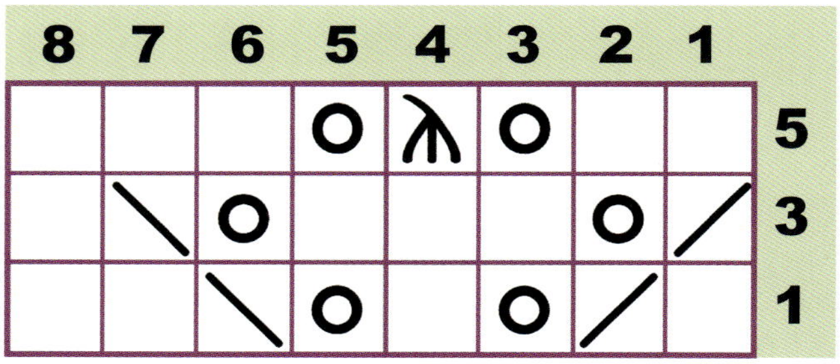

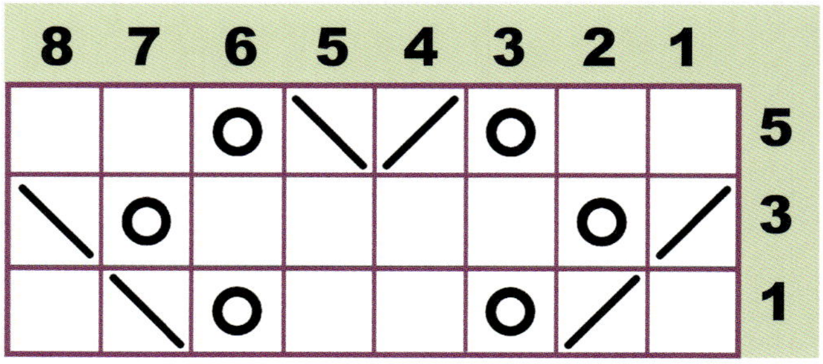

incorporating other stitches

Just because you're knitting lace does not mean you have to restrict yourself to only lace stitches. Try combining other knitting stitches in with the lace patterning.

Cross stitches by skipping a few stitches, knitting into the next stitch on the left needle without removing the skipped stitches and then knitting into the first stitches as you normally would and then sliding all the stitches off without knitting them again. This will create an elongated stitch on the front of your work.

Combining lace and cables can be gorgeous, knit symmetrically or randomly like the example below. Feel free to incorporate any other stitches beside lace stitches as well. Throw in bobbles and nuppes in the repeats every so often or do a line of twisted or drop stitches to add variety and texture. Accent the holes by placing textured stitches on either side of the yarn-overs symmetrically or include them randomly as you wish. Stitch guides are a great resource for many different knitting stitches and cable motifs to experiment with.

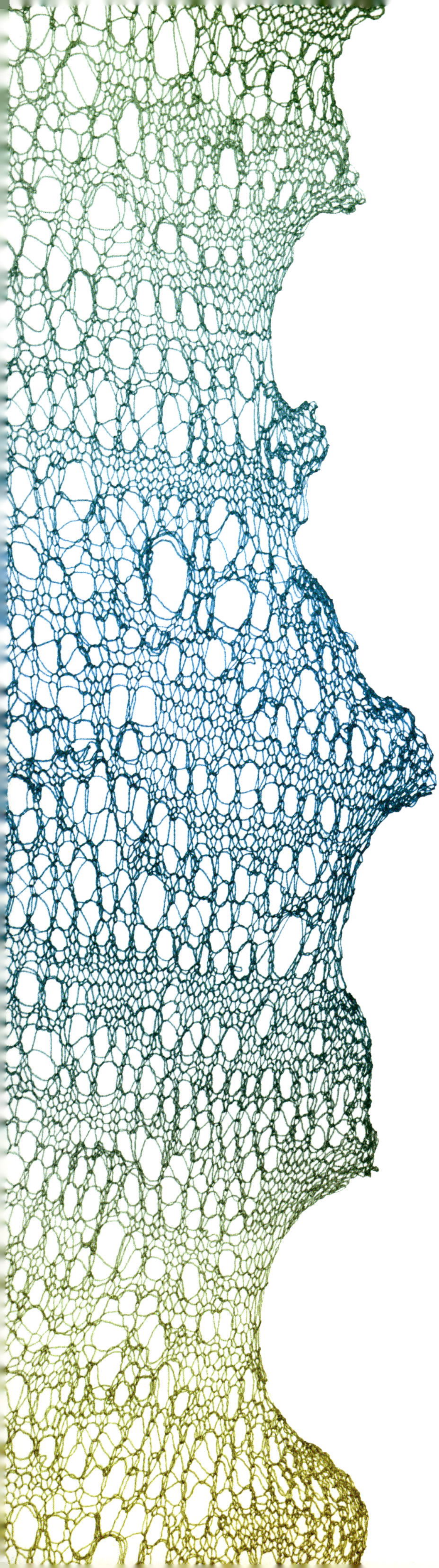

random crazy lace

It's really very easy. You're free to vary the holes and stitches across every single row any way you'd like as long as the final stitch count is maintained for the shape you are making. Keep in mind one simple lace rule: every increase needs a compensating decrease.

In random lace, every row can be completely different. No symmetry is necessary, so there are endless possibilities that evolve as you knit. As an example of a random row, starting with a stitch count of 17, the row could be knit as follows: k2, yo, k1, k2tog, k4, yo, k3tog, yo, p3, k2.

When traveling from one row to the next, consider the direction of the decreases from the previous rows. By continuing the slant from one row to the next in the same direction or by changing direction over a number of rows, you can create abstract patterns and designs with the prominent stitches. Intentionally change the direction of the slant every so often and let lines meander along with the holes. I love watching the lines of decreases undulate in different directions along with the patterns of the holes and changing them as I wish by moving a hole to the left or right on the next row and decreasing in the direction I want it to continue.

To create a nice balance in the overall design, combine lacy areas with large patches of stockinette or garter stitch without holes in some areas. Vary the amount of holes from one area to the next unevenly. Allow the holes to travel from one side to the other, randomly varying the distance between them.

Create full sections of stockinette with few or no holes in some areas and other sections with lots of holes to create a mesh fabric.

completely random
scarf with irregular border
Yarn Place, *Graceful in Irish Lass*
Size 5/3.75mm needles

For an organic feel, create different sized holes in different areas. Separate random sections with ridges of garter or continue the patterning seamlessly as you knit. The fabric will start to speak to you and the spontaneous lace patterning tells you where it wants to go next. Let it take you for a ride.

Mix it up! Use lots of different random, textured stitches along with making holes. Don't forget, yarn-overs can be made on just one or both sides of the fabric.

The overall shape of the piece doesn't have to be perfectly geometric. Create an irregular shape by varying the total amount of stitches in the central portion, in each section or along the sides.

In Part 3 we'll explore irregular borders later that can be incorporated into the main knitting. The real fun of Crazy Lace is watching what happens when you try new things. It's crazy!

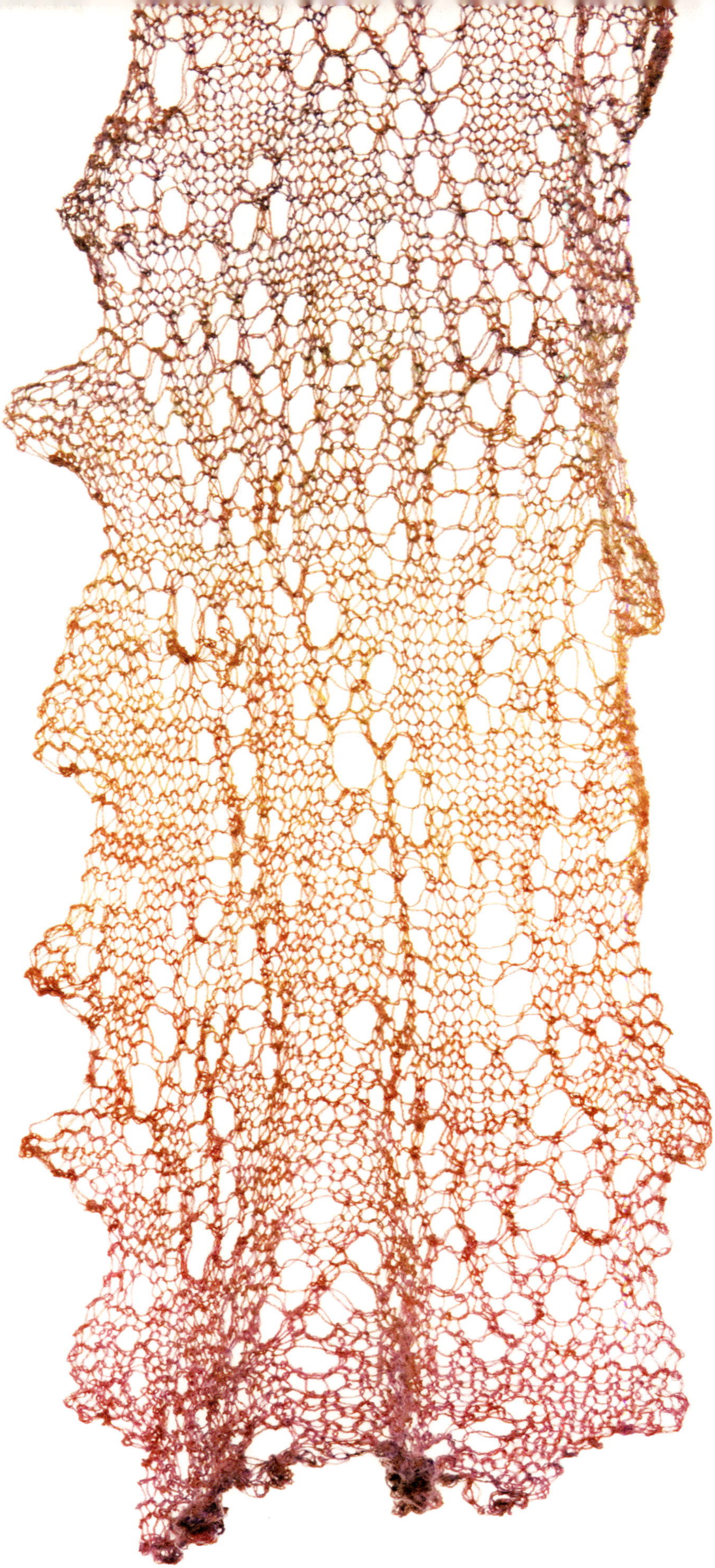

left:
randomly symmetric
swirl circle shawl
Yarn Place, *Gentle*, lacewe ght
overdyed with purple hair-dye
Size 7/4.5 mm needles

right:
random rectangular
scarf with irregular border
Yarn Place, *Graceful in Marooned*
Size 5/3.75mm needles

below:
Yarn Place, *Graceful in Marooned*

nuppes

Nuppes are lovely bobble stitches commonly found in Estonian lace knitting. They are great for Crazy Lace as well. Work them randomly throughout the fabric, alone, in clusters, or symmetrically within each row. To further accent the design, place a knit stitch between the nuppe and the hole.

There are several ways to create a nuppe. One way is to knit into the front and back of the same stitch as many times as you'd like on the right side and purl all of them together on the next wrong side return row. A more traditional approach is to [k1, yo] as many times as you'd like into one stitch, return that group to the left needle immediately and knit them all together through the back loop. Usually a nuppe is a group of 5, 7 or 9 increases in the same stitch, immediately decreased back to a single stitch. Replacing the right needle with a crochet hook makes knitting or purling multiple stitches together much easier.

part 2

the shape of things to come

The wonderful shapes used for making traditional lace shawls follow simple instructions and are a great basis for any Crazy Lace project, whether symmetrical or random. Once you've established which shape you want to make, follow the directions for each shape while improvising within that basic structure. The shapes are created by knitting either in the round or as one flat piece, with increases and/or decreases spaced at regular intervals. Most shapes other than rectangles or squares are usually divided into triangular sections that form the whole; the rate of increase and how many sections you knit determines the shape. usually there is one section per side, i.e. a square has four sections, a pentagon has five and a circle is segmented into eight pie-shaped wedges. Once you determine the shape you want to make, you are free to experiment with the lace between the increases that form the overall shape per row or round.

Since this is creative knitting, this is a perfect time to ask yourself "What if?" What if I increase every fourth row instead of every second row? What if I increase at one edge and not the other? Experiment within the basic instructions and you'll come up with all sorts of interesting shapes!

You may find, depending on the needles you use or the size of your holes and fabric as you progress, that as the shape gets larger you don't need to increase as often as suggested. Try two or three even rows without increases if the fabric starts to warp and pucker too much or the shape is growing wider more quickly than you'd like.

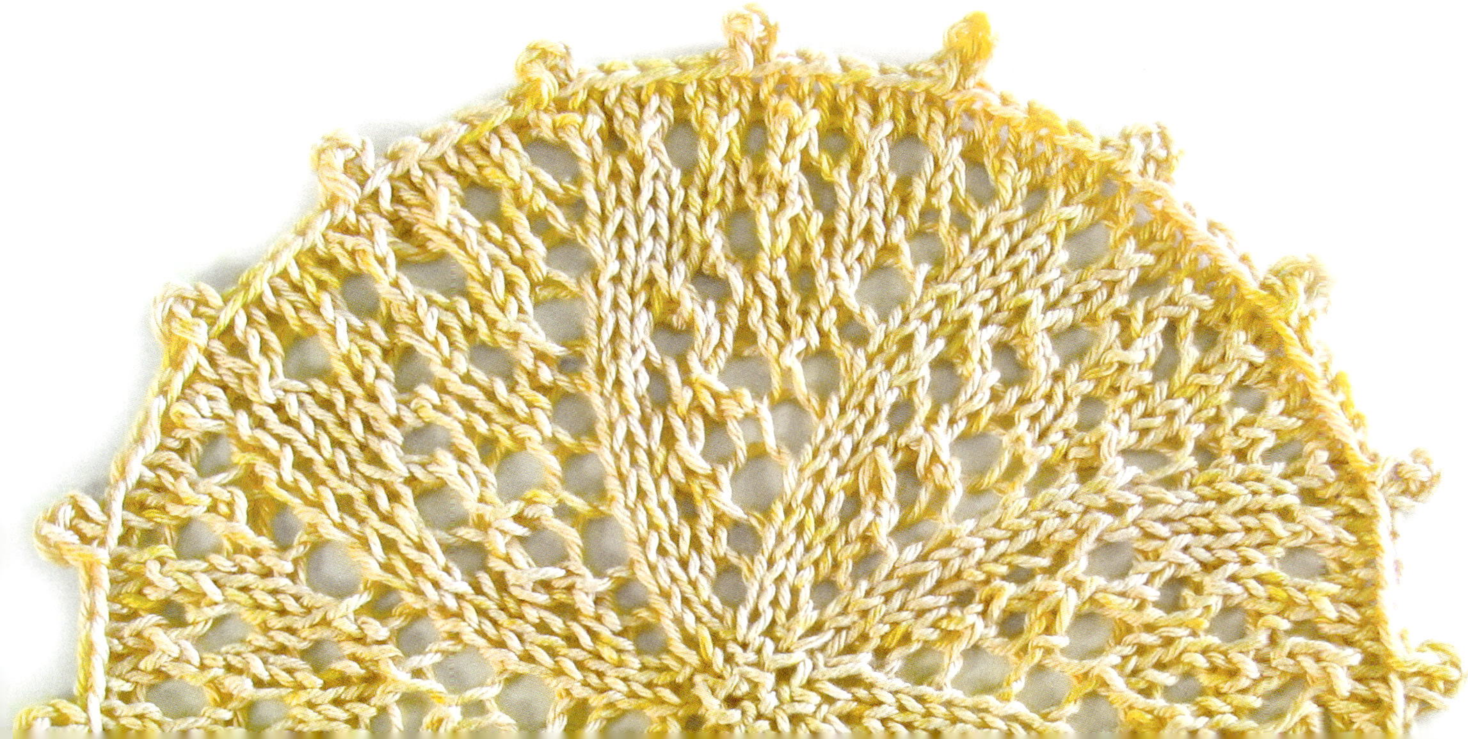

shawls & scarves & stoles, oh my!

Shawls come in all shapes but tend to be square, round or triangular, whereas stoles and scarves are likely to be to be long rectangles. Consider modifying these shapes as well.

As the basic shaping rules are followed, exact gauge isn't terribly important. For pieces created in the round from the center out, determine the size as you knit. For pieces knit flat, a gauge swatch made before beginning determines how many stitches to cast on.

Using the appropriate yarn and needles, knit a gauge swatch following the directions on page 50. Although it is not necessary to duplicate the exact patterning you'll use, try to approximate the overall lace style in order to mimic the final fabric. If you want an airier fabric, go up a needle size or two. If you want something of more substance, do less lace patterning or go down a needle size. Try the swatch again to make sure you're happy with the results.

mixed random and
patterned scarf
with knitted-on borders
Claudia Hand Painted Yarn
Fingering in Indian Turquoise
Size 4/3.5 needles

symmetrically patterned
rectangular shawl
Claudia Hand Painted Yarn
Fingering, original color
removed and overdyed
Size 5/3.5mm needles

squares

The easiest way to make a square is to cast on as many stitches as desired for the width and to knit until the shape is as long as it is wide. You may want to add an all-around border to a square, as in the case of time-honored Shetland shawls.

A fun variation on a square is to knit it from the center out in four equal segments. Use five double-pointed needles, one for each side plus one for knitting. (Of course, you may use one long circular or two circular needles if you prefer.)

Mary Thomas suggests knitting into the back of the stitch on the first round of any shape that starts from the inside out to keep the center flat.

rectangles

Using either a provisional or a crochet cast-on for a flexible edge, cast on any number of stitches you desire for the width of your piece, keeping in mind that it will grow about thirty percent. If you are knitting from a chart or using a specific repeat, make sure you have the correct multiple plus four stitches, two for the selvedge on each end of each row.

Continue to knit, adding lace patterning as desired. To keep the shape geometric, keep the total stitch count between the markers the same for the entire length of the piece.

To create an irregular rectangle, gradually increase and decrease over a number of rows on either side to gently undulate the shape from side to side. Feel free to do different increases and decreases on each end of the row.

Bind off very loosely. Use a crocheted bind-off to keep the edge stretchy or thread all of the stitches on the last row onto waste yarn, block the piece to the desired shape and let it dry, and then bind off. Add a separate edging to either end if desired.

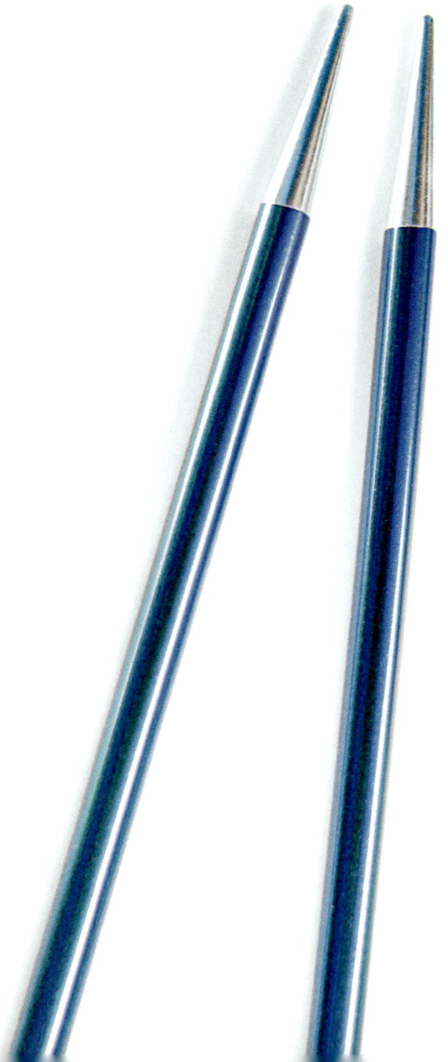

center-out square

knit in the round

Cast on 4 stitches. Kfb each stitch and distribute two of them to each of four needles or divide evenly on circular needles. Prepare for working in the round, being careful not to twist the first round.

Rnd 1 (RS): Knit.

Rnd 2 and all even-numbered Rnds: Work evenly without increases.

Rnd 3: Kfb each stitch to double the number of stitches. (16 stitches)

Rnd 5: K1, (yo, k2, yo, k1) 4 times. (21 stitches)

> Note: If you are using the magic loop/circular method, place markers between the repeats so that you'll have two sections on each side of the needle.

Rnd 7 and all odd Rnds: Continue to increase with a yo after the first stitch and before the last stitch on each needle (or in each section), placing your lace patterning within each section. You'll be increasing a total of eight stitches (two for each side of the square) every increase round.

Transfer the stitches to a circular needle when they outgrow the double-pointed needles, making sure to mark the beginning and end of each side of the square and the beginning of the round with a different color marker. Continue until the square is the desired size.

outside-in mitered square

knit flat

Cast on any number that is double the number of stitches desired for one side, plus 3 stitches for the center decrease.

Row 1 (RS): Work even.

Row 2: Work to center 3 stitches, double decrease (sl 1, k2tog, psso or p3tog), work to end. Because the decreases happen in the center, the patterning will slant inward.

Repeat Rows 1 and 2, placing lace patterning on either side of the centered double decrease, until 3 stitches remain. Decrease all 3 stitches and fasten off.

Pin all four corners and across the sides when blocking to create a square shape with sharp corners.

diamond or diagonal square

knit flat

Cast on 3 stitches.
Row 1 (RS): Kfb, k1, kfb.
Row 2 and all even-numbered rows: Work even.
Row 3 and all odd-numbered rows: Kfb, work to last stitch, kfb.
Continue to increase one stitch at each end of every other row until piece is desired width ending with a right side row.
Then decrease rows as follows:
Dec Row 1: Sl1, k1, psso, k to last 2 stitches, k2tog.
Row 2 and all even-numbered Rows: Work even.
Repeat decrease every other row until 3 stitches remain, k3tog; fasten off.

Pin at all four corners to create a diamond or a square shape with 90 degree angles, depending on how you block it.

triangles

Triangular shawls can be created a number of ways. Most often, the triangle begins with a cast-on of 1-3 stitches, then grows wider with increases spaced at specific intervals. The shape of the triangle varies based on the intervals. If the increases are placed every other row the triangle will expand faster than if the increases are done every fourth row.

tip-to-top horizontal triangle

knit flat

Cast on 1 stitch.
Row 1 (RS): Kfb.
Row 2 and all even-numbered Rows: Work even.
Row 3: Kfb twice. (4 stitches)
Row 5: K1, yo, k2, yo, k1.
Mark the right side of your knitting clearly. All increases are worked on the RS rows.
Row 7: K2, yo, work even to last 2 stitches, yo, k2.

Continue to increase after the first 2 stitches and before the last 2 stitches every other row until the triangle is the desired width.

tip-to-top with center increases

knit flat

This method creates a triangle with a rounded top edge, with the sides slanting toward the center.

Cast on 3 stitches.
Set-up: Purl.
Row 1(RS): K1, yo, k1, yo, k1.
Row 2 and all even-numbered rows: Work even.
Row 3: K2, yo, PM, k1, PM, yo, k2.
Row 5 and every odd-numbered Row: Work even to first marker, yo, slip marker, k1, slip marker, yo, work in lace patterning to end.

Continue to increase before and after center stitch every third or fifth row to keep the top edge angle wider than 90 degrees.

top-down wide triangle

knit flat

This makes a wider triangular shape.

Cast on 3 stitches.
Set-up: Knit.
Row 1(RS): K1, yo, k1,yo, k1. (5 stitches)
Row 2 and all even-numbered Rows: Work even.
Row 3: K1, yo, k1, PM, k1, PM, k1, yo, k1. (7 stitches)
Row 5 and all odd-numbered Rows: K1, yo, knit to first marker, yo, slip marker, knit center stitch, slip marker, yo, knit to last st, yo, k1.

Continue to increase after the first stitch, before and after the center stitch and before the last stitch on every other row until desired size.

symmetrically random
triangular shawl
Plymouth Yarn,
Baby Alpaca Lace
Size 5/3.75 mm needles

circles

A circular shawl can be made using the same concept as the center-out square, segmented like a sliced pie into eight sections. Each section has one or more increases that expands the circle evenly.

Another wonderful way to create a circular shawl was developed by knitting pioneer Elizabeth Zimmerman. The "Pi Shawl", based on the mathematical Pi principal, increases as concentric circles rather than as segments. The Pi Shawl is perfect for incorporating specific patterns. By not having to increase regularly between segments, you have the chance to experiment with stitch patterns that span several rounds.

swirl circles

knit in the round

Cast on 4 stitches.

Set-up Rnd: Kfb each stitch. (8 stitches) Distribute two stitches to each of four double-pointed needles, or divide evenly on circular needles. Prepare for working in the round, being careful not to twist the first round.

Rnd 1: Knit.

Rnd 2: Kfb each stitch. (16 stitches)

Rnd 3 and all odd-numbered Rnds: Work even.

Rnd 4: [K1, yo, k1, PM] 8 times. (24 stitches)

Rnd 6: [K1, yo, k2] 8 times. (32 stitches)

Continue to increase by adding one yo after the first stitch in each section on every other round. Change to circular needles as the diameter grows.

starburst circle
knit in the round

Cast on 4 stitches.
Set-up Rnd: Kfb each stitch. (8 stitches) Distribute 2 stitches onto each of 4 double-pointed needles or divide evenly on circular needles; join being careful not to twist.
Rnd 1: Knit.
Rnd 2: Kfb each stitch. (16 stitches)
Rnd 3 and all odd Rnds: Work even.
Rnd 4: [K1, yo, k1, PM] 8 times. (24 stitches, 8 sections)
Rnd 6: [K1, yo, k1, yo, k1] 8 times. (40 stitches, 2 increases per section)

Continue to add 2 stitches in each section every other round, one after the first stitch and one before the last stitch in each section. Change to circular needles as the diameter grows.

Block to starburst shape by pulling out each of the 8 corners and pinning.

concentric circles, easy as PI

knit in the round

Cast on 6 stitches. Distribute 2 stitches onto each of 3 double-pointed needles or divide evenly on circular needles; join being careful not to twist.

Rnd 1: Knit.
Rnd 2: Kfb each stitch. (12 stitches)
Rnds 3-5: Work even.
Rnd 6: Increase 1 stitch for every stitch, using either kfb or yo between stitches. (24 stitches)
Rnds 7-11: Work even.
Rnd 12: Rep Rnd 6. (48 sts)
Rnds 13-23: Work even.
Rnd 24: Rep Rnd 12. (96 sts)
Rnds 25-47: Work even.
Rnd 48: Rep Rnd 24. (192 sts)

Change to circular needles as the diameter grows. Continue to work evenly, doubling the number of rounds that occur before the previous increase round until the shawl is the desired size.

top-down semi-circles
knit flat

Cast on 2 stitches.
Set-up: Kfb twice. (4 stitches)
Row 1 (RS): [Kfb, PM] 3 times, kfb last stitch. (8 stitches, 4 sections)
Row 2 and all even-numbered Rows: Work even.
Row 3: [Kfb, yo, k1] 4 times. (16 stitches).
Row 5: [K1, yo, k to 1 stitch before marker, yo, k1] 4 times.
Rows 6 - 8: Work even.

Continue to increase after the first stitch and before the last stitch in each section every 4 or 6 rows until the semi-circle is as wide as desired.

other shapes

Other geometric shapes can be knitted from the center out using a method similar to that described for the center-out square and circle. Most can be achieved with symmetrical increases (two stitches per section every other row) or swirl (one stitch per section every other row), following the general rule of thumb:

Cast on one or two stitches for each side of the shape. Join for working in the round. On the first round, knit front and back of each stitch to double the number of stitches. Separate each section with stitch markers. If you are using double-pointed needles, use one needle per side, plus one for knitting. Change to circular needles when the diameter of the piece permits, placing markers between each section as you knit the stitches onto the circular needle.

Mary Thomas' *Book of Knitting Patterns* has instructions for a number of other shapes including pentagons, hexagons and octagons.

By changing the rate of increase, the shape of the semi-circle changes. The pink semi-circle is formed by increasing two stitches per section every other row four times and then every four rows two times.The golden semi-circle is formed by increasing two stitches every other row seven times and then every four rows two times.

blocking is like magic!

Blocking a finished piece is so exciting. The lace pattern blooms to its full beauty when the piece is finished properly. Lace knitting tends to scrunch up as it's knit, so even a light blocking makes a big difference in how the final fabric appears. I love blocking a piece after I'm done to see what secrets are hiding in the patterning.

The first thing to decide is where you're going to block your lace. You'll need a sturdy surface such as a dining room table or bed in the guest room. Foam-core board or foam interlocking blocks for children's flooring make an excellent flat base. Cover any surface with towels to protect it from moisture and/or heat. large, folding blocking boards made especially for knits are available from specialty knitting suppliers.

There are two basic methods of blocking: wet blocking and steam blocking. For large pieces, wet blocking will always be the best choice. Soak the finished lace in a sink or basin of lukewarm water until it has absorbed the water thoroughly and evenly. Squeeze out the excess water as much as possible without wringing the fabric; twisting the fabric will distort the stitches and ruin the fine weave of the lace. When using a heavier yarn, you may need to dry it a bit more. Roll the lace in a towel and squish it under your feet to remove the excess water. Now lay the damp lace onto the toweled surface and carefully stretch it into the proper shape, smoothing it with your hands. Have a yardstick or tape measure handy to measure the piece at different points and make sure the sides are even if the piece is geometric.

The most wonderful part about wet blocking is that you have the opportunity to remold the overall shape into the exact shape you want. If the edges of a rectangle are irregular, correct them at this point by stretching them into the desired shape. Pin each point and peak of a border to their proper shapes with rust-proof pins. I find it easiest to wet block on a towel-covered bed and pin directly into the towels and bedding. Allow the piece to dry completely. Some yarns take longer to dry than others, so check the towels under the lace to make sure they're thoroughly dry as well.

To steam block you will need a good iron that produces steam without dripping. Since most consumer irons tend to drip, it's worthwhile to invest in commercial tailor's iron.

A hand steamer can be used for small pieces. Make sure the surface under the towels is protected as steam will damage wood and some carpets. Hover the steamer or iron an inch or two

above the fabric. If your iron has a 'shot of steam button', give it a couple shots without touching the surface. Otherwise just hover for a few seconds. Be sure to let the fabric cool slightly. Before cooling completely, you can use your fingers to straighten an edge or pull out a corner or point a bit more. I like the combination of wet blocking followed by steaming the best. The final blast of steam really sets the lace stitches.

With either blocking method, the amount a piece is stretched while blocking will completely change the look of the lace patterning. Steam blocking generally doesn't stretch the lace as much as wet locking, so anything that needs a substantial blocking should be wet blocked first followed by a hit of steam.

Sometimes it's necessary to re-block a piece that hasn't been worn in a while. Some fibers have a tendency to shrink back toward their pre-blocked state, especially if they include nylon. A light steam blocking will restore the lace to its full glory.

Note: Unless you want to "kill" your creation, never, ever put your iron directly onto the surface of fiber that contains nylon or acrylic. The heat will permanently melt the synthetic fibers and further blocking will be impossible. On the other hand, sometimes deliberately killing your knitting will be the only way to achieve the desired softness and drapiness. Experiment on a swatch, as once a piece is killed it is irreversibly dead.

part 3

dancing around the edges

Borders add interest to any design and can be approached several ways. Form the border of an angled shape symmetrically by mirroring the shaping on each side or allowing each side to evolve organically by increasing and decreasing randomly over the rows. With Crazy Lace, nothing has to match!

Borders can be knit at the same time as the main piece when knitting a flat square or rectangle. When you begin to knit the first row, place a marker after the number of stitches desired for the right border edge, knit across to an equal (or not!) number of stitches at the end of the row, place a marker and knit the last stitches. Now that the border stitches are delineated, treat the border stitches as a separate area, shaping as desired while knitting the main piece.

For subtle shaping, increase and decrease a couple of stitches at each edge over a few rows. To create a soft curve, separate the increase and decrease rows with several rows of knitting. For a saw-toothed edge, allow the edge to increase over several rows, then bind off the additional stitches on one row.

To create a radically changing edge, (Extreme Crazy Lace!) cast on and bind off stitches along each edge. Consider separating the body from the border by making a eyelet, [yo, k2tog], between them every other row at the border marker.

For shapes that grow from the center, the last few inches can be treated as the border areas by using a different pattern. A Feather and Fan stitch (see page 95, top chart) will create a lovely, undulating edge.

Borders can also be made separately and attached to any shape in a variety of ways. The most simple method is to create the border as a separate piece; cast on a few stitches and knit one side straight while varying the other side to create a decorative edge. Knit until the blocked length of the straight edge matches the blocked length of the edge it will join. Bind off loosely and sew the straight edge to the side of the main piece.

For a rectangular scarf or shawl, try creating a border before the main area is started. Knit a border with a straight top edge the desired width of the piece. Bind off on the wrong side, leaving the last stitch on the needle. Turn the work 90 degrees and with the right side of the border facing, pick up stitches evenly along the straight side of the border. Continue to knit the body of the piece; the border will already be attached on one end.

Knit two separate pieces in this manner, leaving the last row of each side on the needles. Join by grafting or three needle bind-off.

ethereal random triangular shawl,
border knitted onto bound-off edge
Claudia Hand Painted Yarn
Kid Mohair in Whisper

Cast on the required number of stitches to start the border and knit one row.

Before beginning a right side row of the border, slip one stitch from the body onto the left needle knitwise.

Pass the first border stitch over the slipped stitch and transfer that stitch to right needle.

The border is now attached to the edge of the main piece. Continue to work across the wrong side to the end of the row.

As you knit the border, each row will be attached to the main piece on the end of the right side row.

Continue in this manner until all stitches from the body have been worked. Bind off.

Another method of attaching a border is to knit it into live stitches at the beginning and/or end of a piece, creating a seamless transition from the border to the main piece.

- Place the last row of stitches on waste yarn and block the shape to the desired size.

- Return all of the live stitches to the needle.

- On another needle, cast on for the border and knit 1 row.

- Follow the directions on the page 86 to secure the border to the edge.

At each corner of an angled shape, you will have to ease the border around the edge. The easiest way to do this is to increase enough stitches to turn the corner each time you reach it for several rows.

You can use a similar method to knit a border onto a piece that's already been bound off. Begin by casting on the stitches for the width of the border. Pick up a stitch from the bound off edge of the main piece and knit it together with the first stich of the straight edge of the border every other row. You may not need to pick up every bound off stitch to get your border to lay flat. You may pick up th same stitch two times or more to get a ruffled border. For more on ruffling, see page 89.

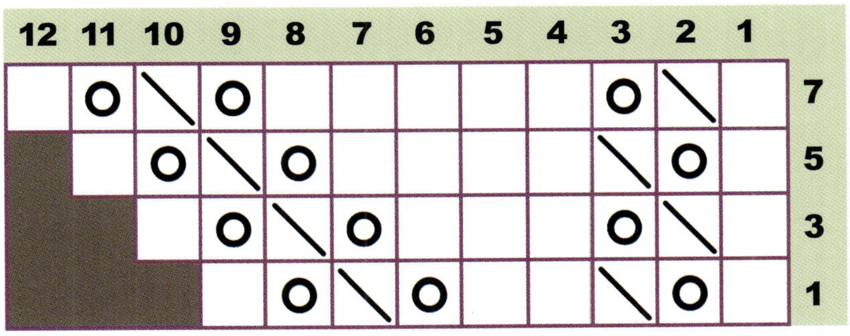

Chart for saw-toothed edging shown below.

symmetrically random
semi-circle shawl
Lion Brand *Moonlight Mohair* and
handpainted chunky mohair
Size 8/5 mm needles

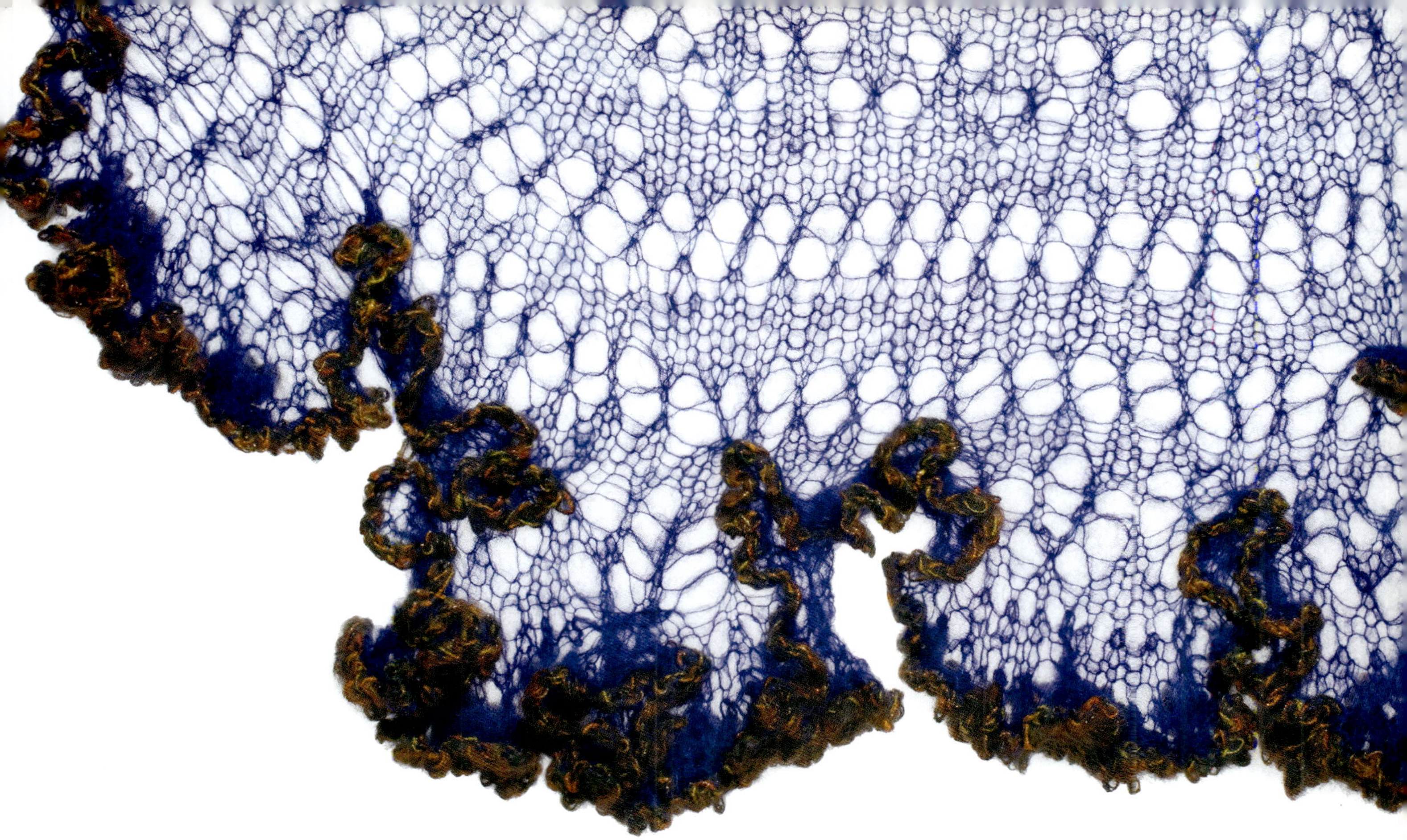

ruffling and ruching around

After your lace fabric is complete, there's a whole world of embellishments that you can add. Ruffles or flowers can really make a piece of lace sing. Add ruffles after the flat work is finished and before the last row of stitches are bound off, or knit them separately and sew them on. Pick up stitches on the edges or on the surface itself and knit ruffles wherever you'd like. Create a surface embellishment of a massive, many-rowed ruffle to swing and swirl over the flat areas.

To create a ruffle, start with any number of cast-on or picked up stitches and increase each stitch in each row over several rows by at least 2 or 3 stitches. The more stitches that are increased, the more ruffled the edge will be. Increases can also be made by placing a yarn-over between each stitch. Experiment with different amounts of increases over several rows to create different sized ruffles.

Hyperbolic shapes are another way to describe ruffles, based on the number and rate of increases and decreases. Rows of even knitting between increase rows create a larger ruffle and soften the hyperbolic effect. The ruffle doesn't take form until after the bind-off which should be loose to keep the edge flexible. For an interesting surprise try increasing more than one stitch at any point along the row.

Go Rufflenutz™ and see what happens!

Ruching is another terrific way to embellish lace. To create a gathered and rippled surface, thread a tapestry needle with matching or contrasting yarn and baste randomly through the finished fabric, than tighten the basting. To create bubbles that resemble Shibori knitting, baste in a circle, then tighten the basting and knot the two ends together. Weave in the ends by forming duplicate stitches. Puff out the bubble. Gathering the edges or meandering a line of ruching in different places creates a wonderfully textural effect. Light, fluffy yarns like mohair work wonderfully for this technique.

Most embellishments do not need to be blocked since the desired affect is usually textural. I like to block the main piece and add the embellishments and ruffles after the blocking to enhance the overall fabric without flattening out the added touch.

I love combining crochet with knitting and I really think the two are invaluable needlearts to learn and use together. There are so many more possibilities for creativity when both are used. A crocheted picot bind-off is a lovely finish for any lace project. As a rule of thumb, use a crochet hook one size larger than the needles to keep the edge loose. Any decorative crochet stitch can be used as the final edge after the piece is bound off. At any point while knitting, slip a stitch from the needle onto a crochet hook and create a crocheted bobble or other decorative stitch right into the surface of the piece. Replace the final loop onto the knitting needle and continue to knit.

Crocheted or knitted flowers, beads and buttons can also be added as final embellishments. Whenever desired, place a bead onto a steel crochet hook that fits through the hole, hook the next unworked stitch and slide the bead from the hook onto the stitch. Replace the stitch onto the left needle and continue knitting. The bead will appear within the lace pattern.

There's a whole world of fun after your basic shape is done. The **Crazy**Lace world definitely isn't flat!

ruffled flower

Cast on 10 stitches
Row 1 (RS): Kfb all stitches. (20 sts)
Row 2: Purl.
Row 3: [K1, yo] to last stitch. (39 sts)
Row 4: Purl
Single crochet bind-off. Twist into desired shape and secure with a couple stitches from the tail.

lace patterns

5 stitch repeats

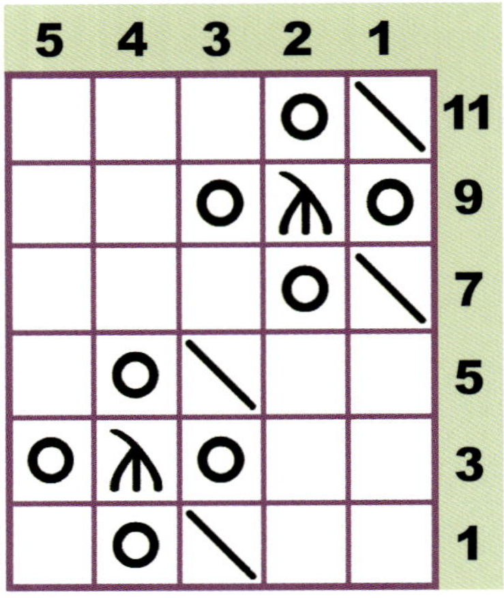

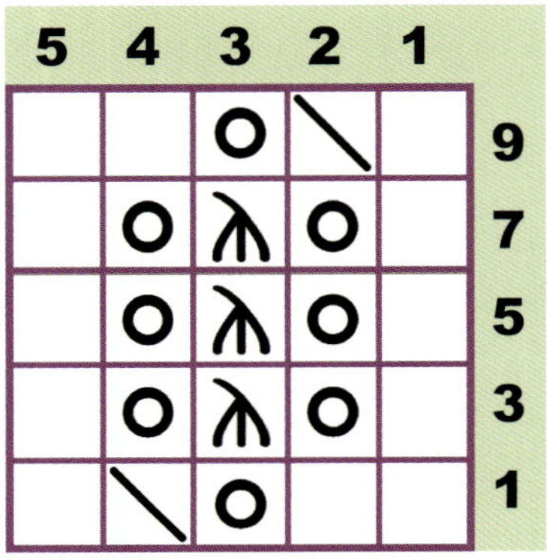

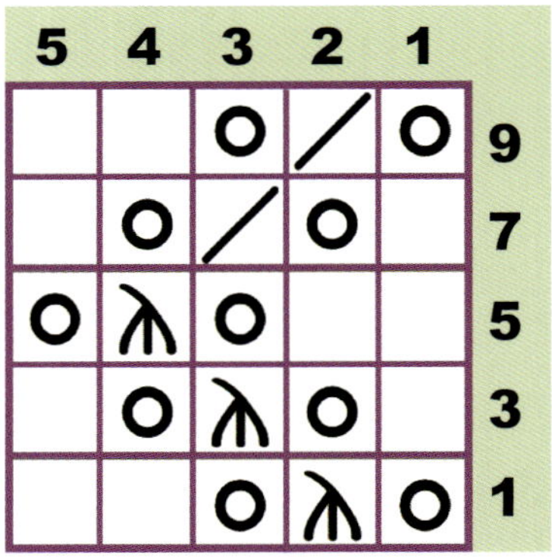

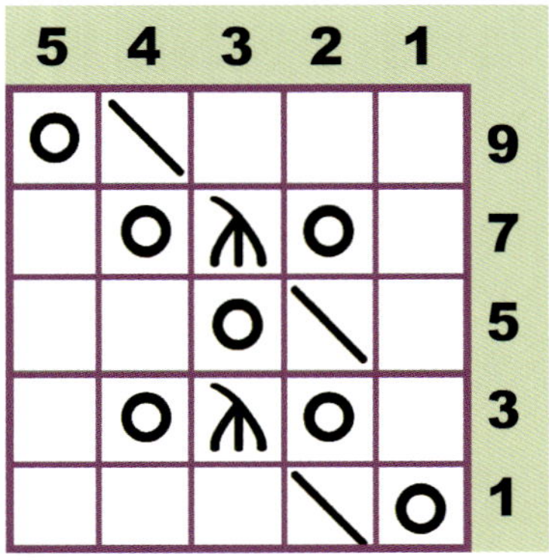

6 stitch repeats

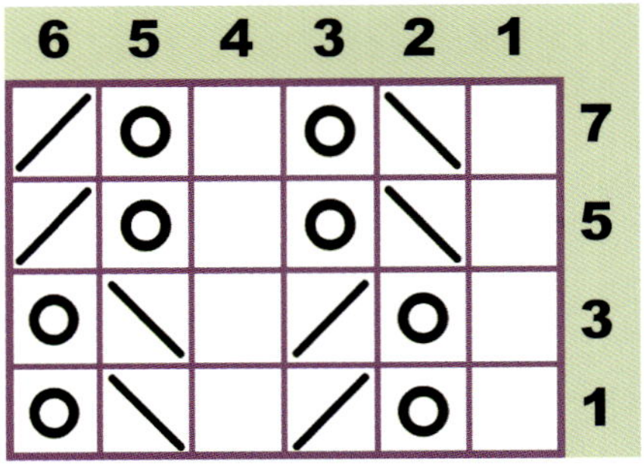

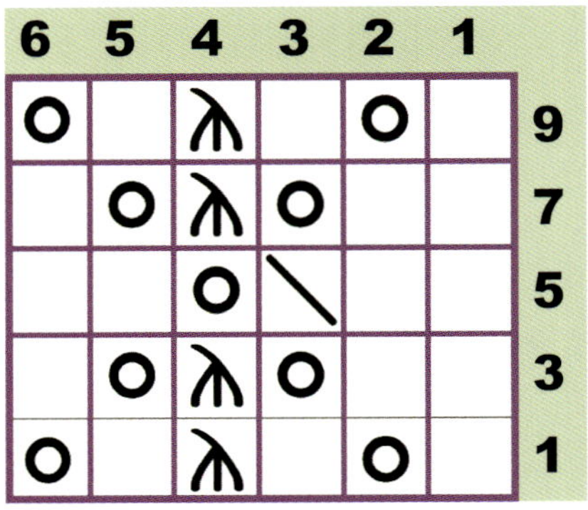

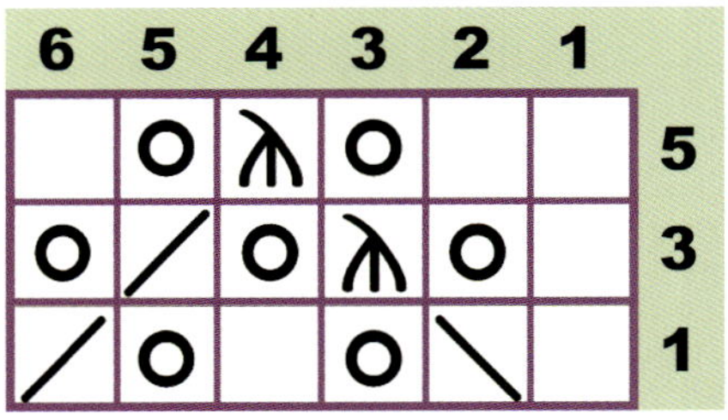

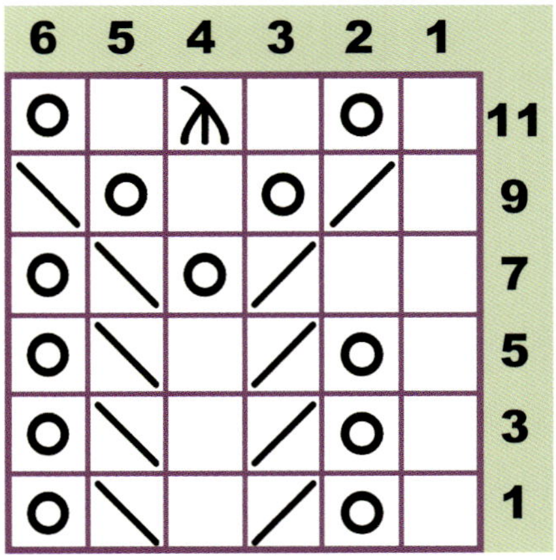

7 stitch repeats

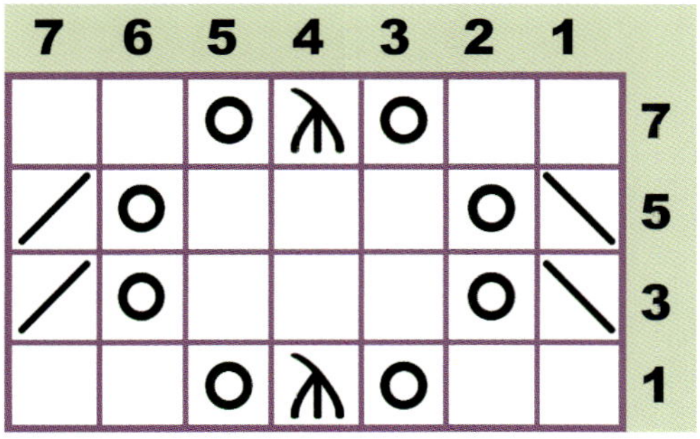

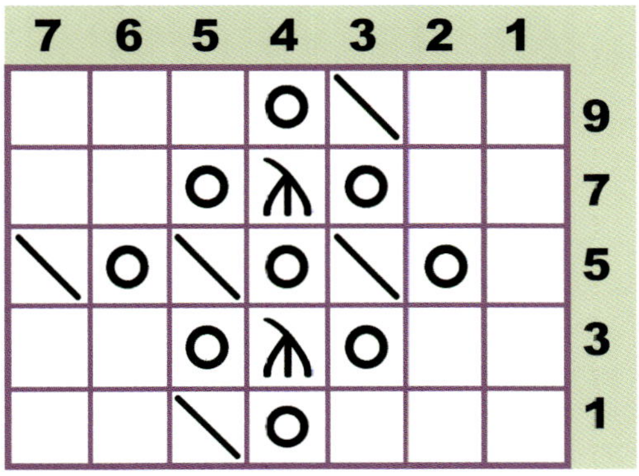

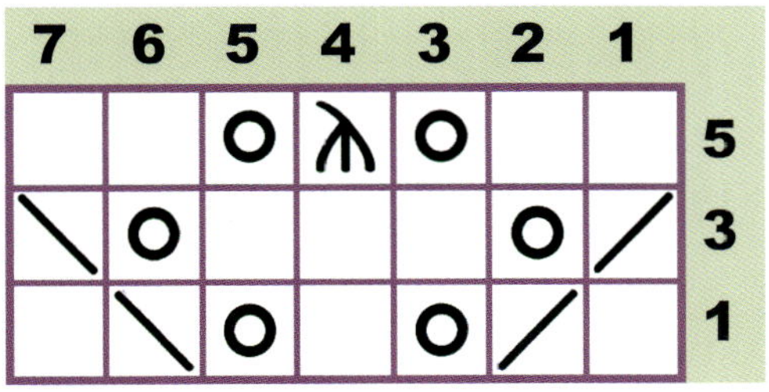

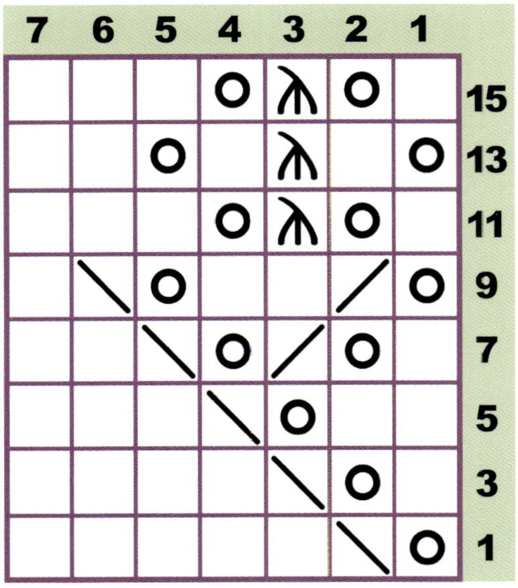

8 stitch repeats

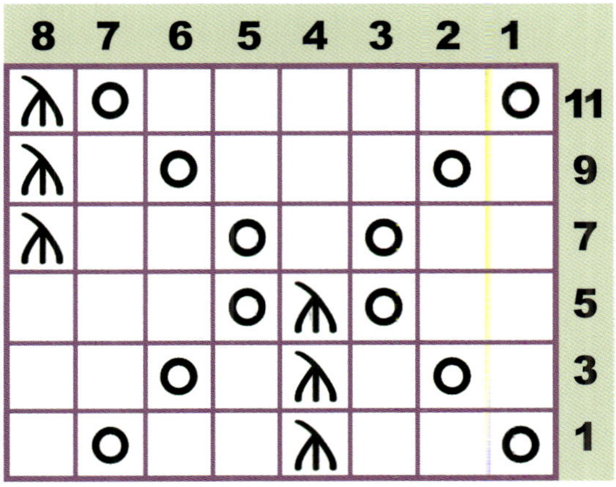

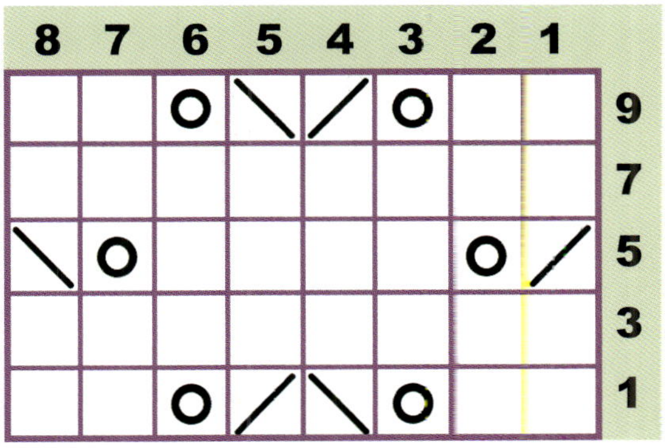

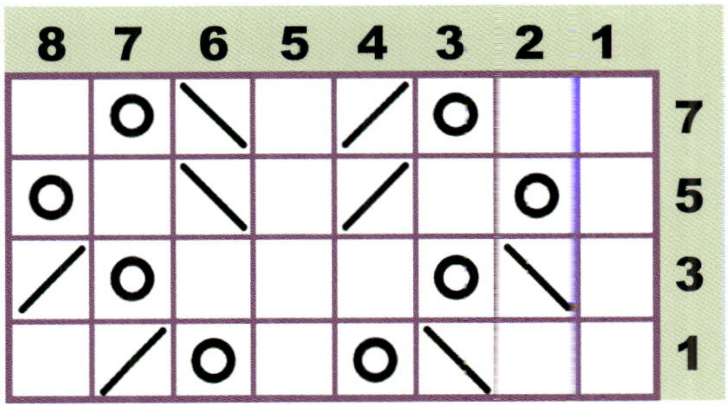

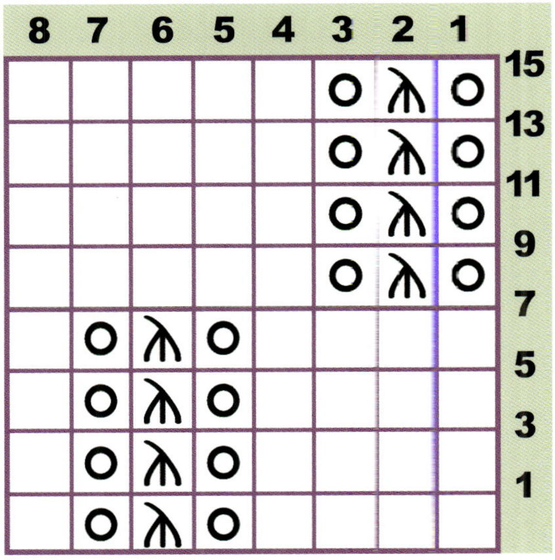

9 stitch repeats

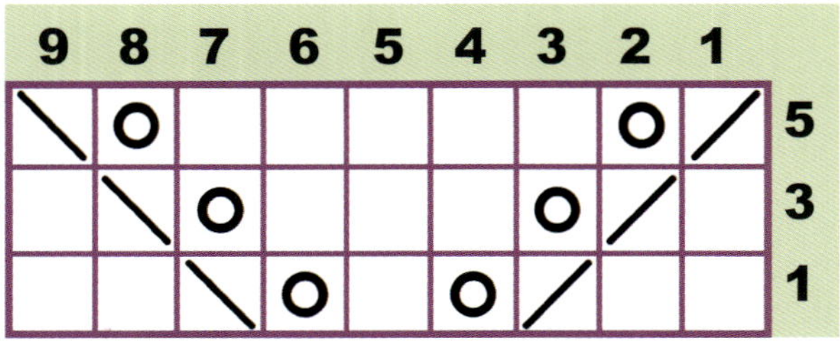

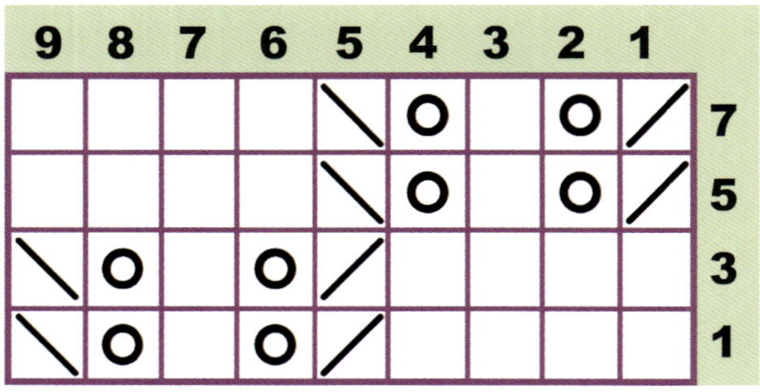

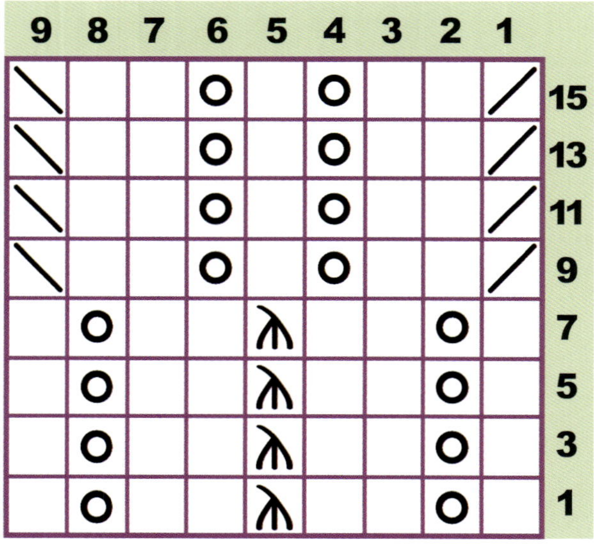

10 stitch repeats

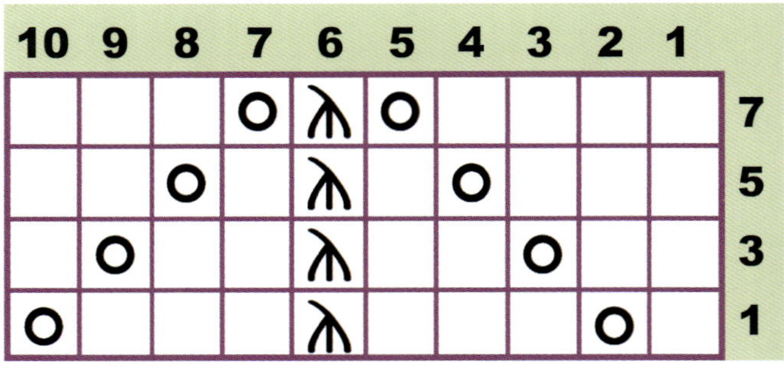

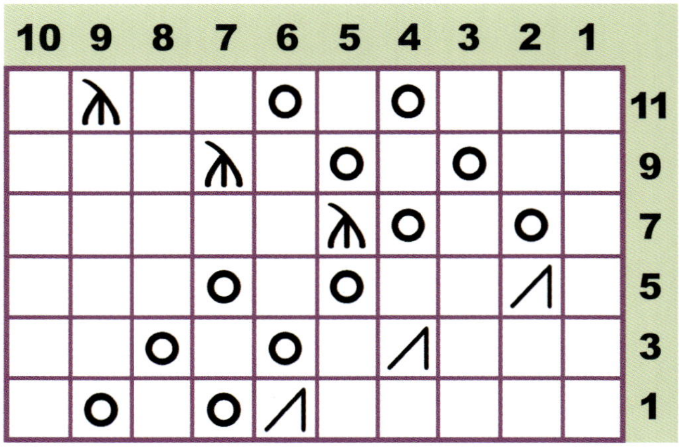

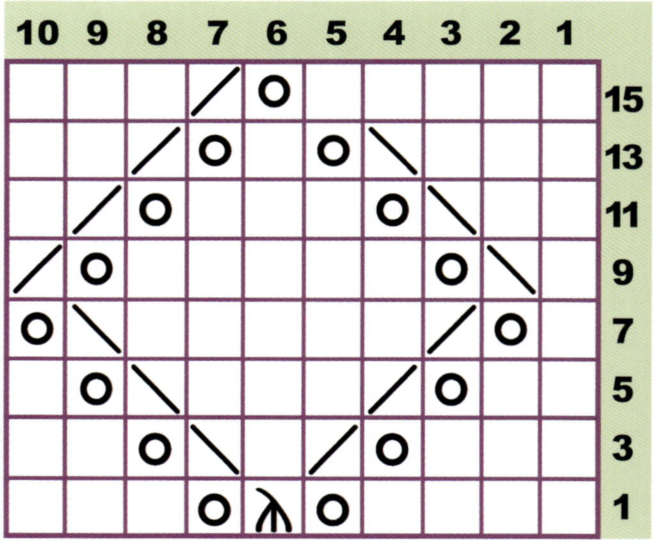

legend

- p: purl
- yo: yarn over
- k: knit
- k2tog: knit two together
- ssk: slip the first st knitwise, sl the next st purlwise, knit both slipped sts tog
- k3tog: knit 3 together
- k3tbl: knit 3 together through back loop
- sk2p: slip 1, knit 2 together, pass slip stitch over

11 stitch repeats

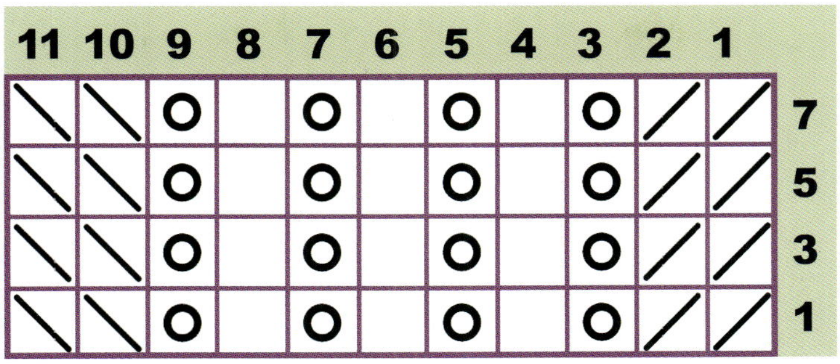

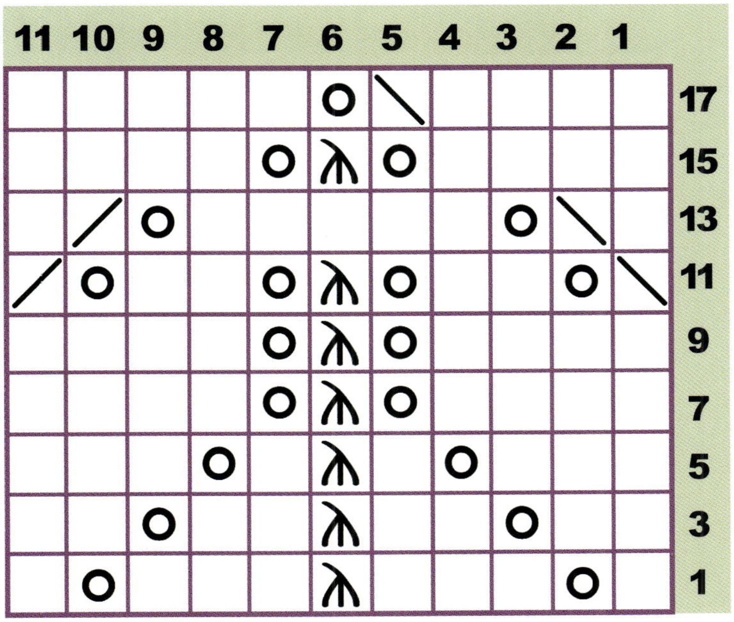

12 stitch repeat

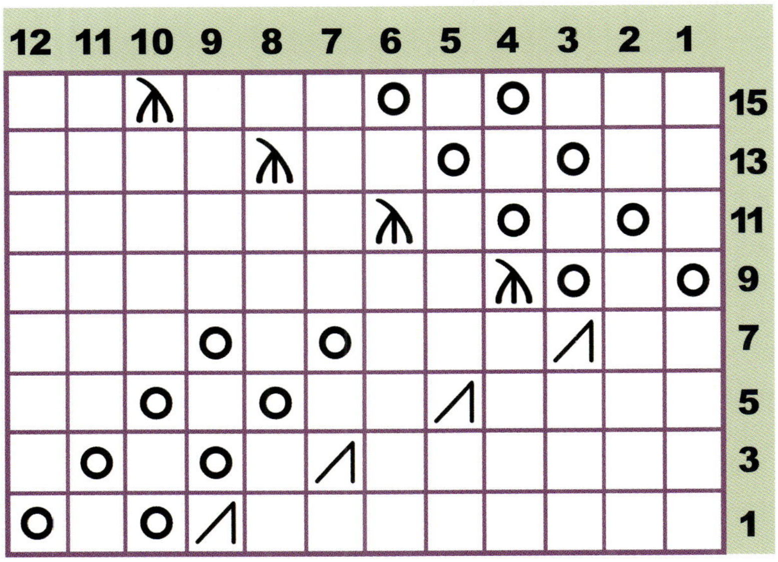

resources

yarn

I would like to thank Claudia of Claudia Hand Painted Yarn, Feza Yarns and Yarn Place for providing some of the yarn used in this book.

- Claudia Hand Painted Yarns, Fingering www.claudiaco.com
- Feza Yarns, Alp Light www.fezayarns.com
- Knit Picks, Shine Sport www.knitpicks.com
- Yarn Place, Graceful www.yarnplace.com
- Yarn Place, Adagio www.yarnplace.com
- JoJoland, Harmony www.jojoland.com
- JoJoland, Melody www.jojoland.com
- Curious Creek Fibers, Wasonga www.curiouscreek.com
- Malabrigo, Lace www.malabrigoyarn.com

needles

- Knitpicks, Options Interchangeable Harmony Wood www.knitpicks.com
- Addi, Lace Circular Needles www.addineedleshop.com
- Signature Needles, Stiletto Points www.signatureneedlearts.com

software

Knit Visualizer www.knitfoundry.com/software.html

books

- Gossamer Webs: The History and Techniques of Orenburg Lace Shawls by Galina Khmeleva
- Knitted Lace of Estonia: Techniques, Patterns, and Traditions by Nancy Bush
- Traditional Knitted Lace Shawls by Martha Waterman
- A Gathering of Lace by Meg Swansen
- Victorian Lace Today by Jane Sowerby
- Knitting Lace Triangles by Evelyn A. Clark
- Creative Knitting: A New Art Form by Mary Walker Phillips
- Harmony Stitch Guides by The Harmony Guides
- Knitting Patterns 300 Lace www.needleartsbookshop.com
- Heirloom Knitting by Sharon Miller
- Mary Thomas' Knitting Book by Mary Thomas

random Rufflerutz™
collar & cuff with
bead embroidered
button closure,
assorted yarns
Size 5, 6 & 7 needles

- A Treasury of Knitting Patterns by Barbara G. Walker
- Creating Original Hand-Knitted Lace by Margaret Stove

other

- highlighter tape www.highlightertapes.com
- lace stitch markers www.ellenshalfpintfarm.com
- brass ring stitch markers www.knitpicks.com
- knitting chart keeper www.knitpicks.com

- Anne Richardson Collection www.arcfashion.com
- Cesar Cuevas Photography www.cesarcuevas.com
- Ellene Warren knit and crochet patterns www.ellenewarren.com

reference

abbreviations

ch: crochet chain

k: knit

k2tog: knit 2 together

k3tog: knit 3 together

kfb: knit into front and back of same stitch

PM: place marker

rep: repeat

rnd: round

RS: right side

sk2p: slip 1, k2tog, pass slipped stitch over

sl: slip

ssk: slip the first stitch knitwise, sl the next st purlwise, knit both slipped sts together

st(s): stitch(es)

WS: wrong side

yo: yarn over

legend

k: knit

p: purl

yo: yarn-over

k2tog: knit 2 together

ssk: slip the first stitch knitwise, slip the next stitch purlwise, knit both slipped sts tog

sk2p: slip1knitwise, k2tog pass slipped stitch over

k3tog: knit 3 together

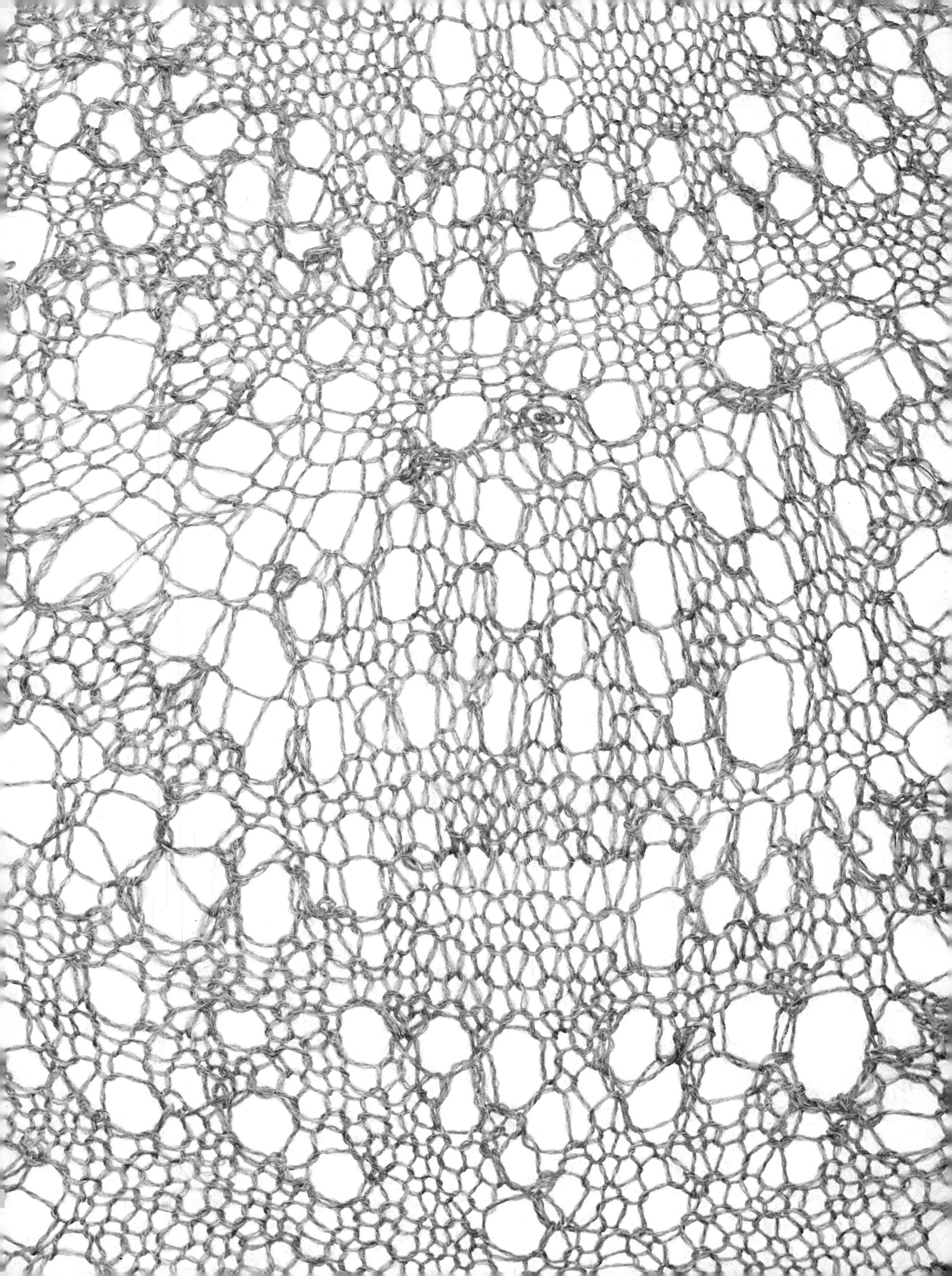